Praise for

What Pain Teaches Us:
Spiritual Lessons from Two Years of Anguish

"Written with sensitivity and warmth, Rabbi Grinblat bares her own terrifying encounter with illness and mortality to shine some light in a very dark experience. With her as our guide, we too can make it through the valley of the shadow with resolve, humanity, and even our humor intact."

- **Rabbi/Dr. Bradley Shavit Artson**
Author, "Lessons from My Cancer,"
Dean, Ziegler School of Rabbinic Studies, American Jewish University

"As Alain de Botton wisely said: '*We should not feel embarrassed by our difficulties, only by our failure to grow anything beautiful from them.*'

Rabbi Ilana has created a beautiful, insightful, spiritual gift from the pain and suffering she experienced. Her memoir is a must-read for anyone who is struggling to navigate a challenging healing journey, or who cares for someone who is.

She speaks with deeply touching vulnerability, with a voice of wisdom that only comes from surviving the descent into pain and darkness with courage and returning to the world with precious treasures to share.

Steeped in Jewish wisdom, there's great relevance for us all, which transcends religion, and resonates deeply with our shared humanity."

- **Kathy Harmon-Luber**
Author, *Suffering to Thriving: Your Toolkit for Navigating Your Healing Journey; How to Live a More Healthy, Peaceful, Joyful Life*

"We can all learn from Rabbi Grinblat's insights born of pain; the deep meaning she finds in our sacred texts as a result, and the comfort she brings to us all through her writing."

- **Rabbi Steve Leder**
New York Times Bestselling Author
Author, *More Beautiful Than Before: How Suffering Transforms Us*

What Pain Teaches Us

ALSO BY ILANA GRINBLAT

Blessings and Baby Steps: The Spiritual Path of Parenthood

Castles and Catch: Spiritual Lessons Children Teach Us

The Viral Spread of Hope: Finding Inspiration in Tough Times

What Pain Teaches Us

Spiritual Lessons from Two Years of Anguish

Ilana Grinblat

Copyright © 2024 Ilana Grinblat

All rights reserved.

ISBN: 9798336041606

Table of Contents

Table of Contents ix

Introduction xvii

Acknowledgements xxi

Author's Note xxiii

Year One 1

Year Two 131

Epilogue 227

Glossary of Jewish Terms: 235

Recommended Resources 239

Index of Torah Portions 241

Endnotes 243

This book is dedicated to
my beloved healers, family, friends, and community.
Thank you for freeing me
from the prison of pain, illness, and suffering.

and especially to my aunt, Susan Mingelgrin,
who died on the day this book was published,
on Tu B'av, the holiday of love,
for her loving, motherly support throughout my life
and for modeling how to endure illness
with grace, humor, and perseverance.
Her life was a love letter
to her/our family and to Israel.
May her memory be a blessing.

A song of ascent: Out of the depths I call You God
Listen to my voice...

- Psalm 130:1-2

I call heaven and earth to witness with you this day:
I have put before you: life and death, the blessing and the curse.
Choose life—so you and your descendants will live.

- Deuteronomy 30:19

The Journey

by Mary Oliver

One day you finally knew

what you had to do, and began,

though the voices around you

kept shouting

their bad advice –

though the whole house

began to tremble

and you felt the old tug

at your ankles.

"Mend my life!"

each voice cried.

But you didn't stop.

You knew what you had to do,

though the wind pried

with its stiff fingers

at the very foundations,

though their melancholy

was terrible.

It was already late

enough, and a wild night,

and the road full of fallen

branches and stones.

But little by little,

as you left their voices behind,

the stars began to burn

through the sheets of clouds,

and there was a new voice

which you slowly

recognized as your own,

that kept you company

as you strode deeper and deeper

into the world,

determined to do

the only thing you could do –

determined to save

the only life you could save.

-Mary Oliver, from *Dream Work*

any point along the way, I would have done whatever it took to escape – but I couldn't.

I had been a rabbi for twenty and a half years when my pain and illness began. In these excruciating months, my spiritual training wasn't much help to me. Like Rabbi Yochanan, I was dependent on others: my doctors, nurses, medical massage therapists, spiritual director, colleagues, family, friends, and community who together pulled me out of the prison. It wasn't as quick as in the story with the rabbis. No one person could unlock the door and let me out right away. Rather, it was more like being trapped in an escape room where each person was part of a team effort. Each friend, therapist, doctor, nurse or ambulance driver, or community member would solve one small piece of a puzzle, which would lead to the next clue, which opened the door to the escape room just a tiny crack further until the door opening was wide enough for me to squeeze my body through it inch by inch. I wasn't free one day in one fell swoop – but extremely slowly, at the pace of a snail, I eventually emerged.

Some days, I thought I had gotten out, only to find a new locked door. But slowly I was pulled out into the sunlight by the care of medical professionals and the love of family, friends, and community. I am eternally grateful to each person who solved a piece of the puzzle for me and who together with others set me free. I offer this book to each of you as a small token of my appreciation.

Indeed, none of us is free of the pain and sufferings of this life which reaches each of us in turn. None of us can free ourselves from the prison of pain. All we can do is pay the kindnesses and love we have received forward to others.

Like Rabbi Hiyya bar Abba and Rabbi Yochanan, my sufferings are not dear to me. I would gladly give back the pain along with any lessons that I learned from it. But I can't. What I can do is thank those who freed me from the prison of suffering, and share the keys I was given, hoping to unlock the prison cell doors for someone else – maybe even for you.

Acknowledgements

August 19, 2024/ 15 Av 5784 (*Tu B'av*: The Holiday of Love)

First and foremost, I thank the medical and healing professionals who cared for me to whom this book is dedicated. They saved my life and pulled me out of many, long months of being in excruciating pain, disabled and homebound. (I have kept some of their names anonymous to protect their privacy.) I am eternally grateful to my healers for saving my life.

Thank you to my family to whom this book is also dedicated: my husband, Tal for your support throughout this torturous ordeal and for your integrity as my/our world fell apart. I am profoundly grateful for our son Jeremy and our daughter, both of whom took care of me during my illness. Thanks to Jeremy for designing and formatting this book and to Hannah for coming up with the title. Thanks to my folks, in-laws, siblings, aunts, uncles, and cousins for their love and support.

Thanks to my dear friends to whom this book is also dedicated. I would especially like to thank my chavruta (friend/study partner) Rabbi Rachel Rudis Bovitz who edited this book and provided helpful feedback throughout. Thanks to all my friends for their emotional support – especially to Dr. Ari Blitz for his medical advice, Kostadis Roussos (who provided helpful feedback on a draft of this book), Deborah Blum (for our walks and for nourishing my body and soul), Carla Ohringer Engle, Roxana Daneshvar Sharifi, Sara Alex Schwatz-Rossi for all our conversations, Mia Pardo (who motivated me to edit the book), Lara Krinsky, Guita Cohen and Julie Weissman for our walks. Thanks to Gidon and the other fellow 5:00 AM swimmers for

Ilana Grinblat

starting my day with joy and to those I met at the workshop with Dr. David Wise courageously sharing their experiences with pelvic pain.

Thanks to my colleagues and friends to whom this book is also dedicated. Thanks to the members of the Board of Rabbis of Southern California for their prayers and support, especially to Rabbi Lori Shapiro who provided me medical, emotional, and spiritual support, Rabbi Ahud Sela who visited me in the hospital, Rabbis Dr. Bradley Shavit Artson and Steve Leder for reading the manuscript and writing blubs, Rabbi Stephen Spiegel, Rabbi Naomi Levy, and many other rabbis for their prayers and support. Thanks to my Open Temple colleagues, Rabbi Lori, Kirsten Hudson and Jayne Bennet, who cared for me when I collapsed at work. Thanks to my colleagues at the Jewish Federation of Greater Los Angeles and to my husband's work colleagues at Lewitt-Hackman for their support.

This book is also dedicated to my communities – the families of Ahavat Torah, Open Temple, Temples Har Shalom, Beth Am, Beth Shalom, B'nai Emet, Nashuva, and Scout Troop 360 for their prayers and support during my illness. Thanks especially to the library minyan members of Temple Beth Am for bringing my family and me food for two weeks when I returned from the hospital and providing housing to Rabbi Stephen Spiegel for many weeks while his wife was in the intensive care at the hospital. Thanks to Kerry Abram of Temple Har Shalom for her wise guidance and our many discussions about healing over Rummikub. Thanks to Kathy Harmon-Luber of Temple Har Shalom for writing the blurb and for her partnership and insights on this healing journey. Thanks to Evan Gilder of Scout Troop 613, for recommending me to serve as chaplain in Philmont. Thanks to congregation Ahavat Torah. I look forward to becoming your rabbi.

I'm grateful to have all these layers of caring and love during my illness and throughout my life. I thank God for life and for sending me all these angels who have saved and enriched my life.

Finally, thanks to my friend, Joel Chassnoff, and to Barry Rosenblatt of the library minyan for asking me what I had learned from this medical crisis. When you asked me, I had not learned anything, but now I have. Joel and Barry, what follows is my answer.

Author's Note

This book recounts the true story of events that happened to me over a two-year period. I have included dates in this book to give a sense of when these events occurred. The date for each chapter is the date when the first event mentioned in that chapter began. Some chapters were written as events were occurring, and some chapters were written later. Therefore, the dates in the book are not necessarily when the chapters were written, just the date that the events described in that chapter began. For some chapters, I have a precise date and for others I don't recall the exact date and have given an approximate date.

Year One

How It All Began

November 8, 2021

I could begin this story when the physical pain began, but to me, this journey started a couple weeks earlier. It started on a sleepless night, after the funeral of a sixteen-and-a-half-year-old named Esther Iris Blum on November 7, 2021.

Esther had been a thriving, loving person – artistic, bright, talented, and cheerful – a dancer, a surfer, a writer, and musician, with a caring family, friends, and community and a beautiful spirit. Twenty-one months into the Coronavirus pandemic, Esther committed suicide.

There is something particularly painful about watching your children bury their friend. It's so excruciating that there should be a special word for this particular flavor of anguish.

Due to the isolation caused by the pandemic, we weren't spending much time with our friends, as we usually did before the pandemic. Before Covid, family friends would invite us over for a meal and we would reciprocate. We would see many of our friends, including the Blum family, every week at synagogue. We would go to the beach, concerts and plays together, and our friendships were nurtured through weekly interactions. With the pandemic, all that natural rhythm of gathering shut down. As a result, although we used to see the Blum family each week, we hadn't seen them for many months. We didn't know that Esther had been struggling with depression. Esther's death came as a complete and utter shock to us and to our community.

Ilana Grinblat

In the few days after we heard the news of Esther's death, my folks, my husband and I each had separate, private conversations with our children, Jeremy and Hannah, who were seventeen and fourteen at the time. We did not coordinate with one another what we would tell the children, and we didn't hear each other's conversations. Nonetheless, we each ended up sharing the exact same message to the children. We all essentially told them: If you're struggling, please tell us. Don't keep your feelings inside. We're here to help. Reach out to us and whatever you're dealing with, we will work it out together. You're not alone. We love you.

Somehow, this message must have gotten through to me as well. The night after Esther's funeral, the house was quiet with my husband and children asleep, but I couldn't sleep. The truth was I was miserable. I had been miserable for a very long time.

When the pandemic struck, I was the Vice-President of Community Engagement for the Board of Rabbis of Southern California at the Jewish Federation of Greater Los Angeles. My job was to be the rabbi for the rabbis – to support the community's rabbis so that they could better support their congregants. The twenty-one months of the pandemic had been a non-stop series of emergencies.

My colleagues had to learn to do their jobs in entirely new ways and use new mediums. We faced questions like: What precautions need to be taken for a funeral of someone who died from the Coronavirus or its complications? What if the surviving family had been exposed? How does one officiate at *b'nai mitzvah* (coming of age) ceremonies when people can't be in the same room together? How do we respond to and prevent antisemitic zoom bombings of religious services? What are the current health department regulations for gathering for funerals, for services? What support do our hospital chaplains need and what do our congregational rabbis and school rabbis need? What precautions do the funeral homes and mortuaries need to take to keep our rabbis safe when officiating at funerals? How can we provide support to congregants who are losing their jobs as a result of the pandemic?

Due to my job, I was at the epicenter of all these questions and much more — frantically relaying information from government officials, funeral homes, community organizations to the rabbis and from the rabbis to these organizations. I was convening support calls with the rabbis at hospitals, congregations, and schools as well as responding to constant questions from colleagues, as the government regulations changed daily on the state and local level.

Since schools and offices had shut down, my children were doing school virtually from home and my husband was practicing law in the dining room twelve hours a day, helping clients who were all facing crises in their businesses due to the pandemic. Our home is fairly small, and there wasn't enough room for each of us to essentially operate four different offices out of our house. While dealing with constant work emergencies, I was trying to help my son with geometry and world history and help my daughter cope with her overwhelming fear of catching Covid. I was striving to help both my family and our community-leaders cope with the manifold ways in which our lives were falling apart, all at once.

The pandemic was only the latest in a series of emergencies. Beforehand were the fires that swept through the area as well as antisemitic shootings at synagogues and attacks on other houses of worship around the world. But the pandemic required emergency response at a whole other level.

Along with the Covid pandemic, the country was grappling with a second pandemic — that of hatred — racism, antisemitism, islamophobia, sexual assault, homophobia, and ableism. All the forms of hatred were reaching a boiling point as the months dragged on and this rage was expressed in many acts of violence.

During these many months of pandemic, I had been trying as hard as I could to help everyone, hoping against hope that things would get better. I had been swimming through wave after wave of disaster, trying to get to calmer waters beyond the waves, but the waves just wouldn't stop coming.

Ilana Grinblat

After twenty-one months of pandemic, I was beyond exhausted, and Esther's death was such a shock that it popped the lid off my emotions. I couldn't contain them anymore.

The night after the funeral, I couldn't sleep for hours and hours, the thoughts were racing through my head. To try to get them out, I wrote a long letter to my husband about everything I was upset about in detail. I even emailed it to him as he slept, so that I couldn't take it back. I had to let out all the pain I had been storing inside for so long.

Only after I emailed the letter at about 4:00 AM was I able to finally fall asleep.

Esther was passionate about many things but above all, Esther was devoted to telling the truth – even painful truths. In the last months of Esther's life, Esther had come out as non-binary to family and friends. Esther had asked to be referred to by the pronoun they/them. Esther was so committed to the truth that they would object to any hint of falsification. When Esther's mother would color her hair, Esther would object, saying: 'You don't have to do that, Mom. You should just show your hair as it is and embrace getting older.' Esther protested even the slightest hint of dishonesty.

Somehow, Esther's commitment to honesty had rubbed off on me that night. I couldn't keep the truth about how devastated I was feeling inside any longer. Thereafter, when anyone asked me how I was feeling, I couldn't lie and say fine anymore. I replied honestly, "I'm a wreck, actually," and I'd explain why. I couldn't pretend to be cheery anymore. Esther's tragic death had blown my cover right off.

At Esther's funeral, Rabbi Adam Kligfeld of Temple Beth Am, shared a poem that Esther had written which had been published in the synagogue's literary magazine a couple months before Esther's death. The poem was about a river. In retrospect the poem was haunting. It expressed honestly the truth of Esther's struggles. In the poem, Esther addressed the river and asked:

> *River, how are you always so happy and cheerful?*
> *Why can't I be like that too?*

Maybe you're not quite
as happy as you seem
although you fall so beautifully
from every cliff you face.
Nobody really knows
if you look over the edge
and feel horribly afraid.

That night, I, too, felt like I was looking over the abyss. I had been trying to hold it together for *so* long – working so hard every moment for my family, my colleagues, and community. I just couldn't hold it together any longer.

In Jewish tradition, the Torah (the Hebrew Bible) is divided into fifty-four parts, and one or two of these parts is assigned to each week of the year. The spiritual premise of Judaism is that the Torah portion of each particular week offers insights about the events in our lives and in our world that week. In Judaism, each week of our lives is lived through the prism of that week's Torah portion.

In the days after Esther's funeral, I wanted to teach about Esther's life and legacy. I looked at the Torah portion of that week and found that it too told the story of a river. It told the tale about how Jacob was about to meet up with his brother Esau who he had run away from twenty years earlier. Jacob had fled for his life, so that his brother wouldn't kill him in rage.

Twenty years later, Jacob was returning home, and on the way, he was poised to meet up with Esau again. Jacob was terrified of being killed by Esau and the four hundred men with him. So, Jacob divided his family into two groups and had them stay in two separate areas lest Esau be able to attack both groups at once. Jacob then crossed the river and spent the night alone wrestling with an angel until the dawn.

That night by the river was a turning point for Jacob. Until that night, Jacob responded to tough situations by lying and fleeing. He deceived his father. He ran away from his brother Esau. He snuck out of his father-in-law Laban's house instead of telling Laban that he was leaving with Laban's daughters and grandchildren. But that night, Jacob changed.

By the river, Jacob wrestled with the angel all night, and as dawn was breaking, the angel begged Jacob to release him, but Jacob said he wouldn't let go until the angel gave him a blessing. So, the angel changed Jacob's name from Jacob, which means crooked, to Israel, which means one who wrestles with God. The next day, when he met Esau again, the encounter was the first time in his life where he confronted a terrifying situation honestly.

Esther's funeral prompted me to have a sleepless night like Jacob did wrestling with my painful feelings. Only once I wrote honestly the letter about my feelings and emailed it to Tal would they release me and let me sleep.

After Jacob's honest encounter with Esau, the Torah recounts that he arrived in Shalem, a city in Shehem in the land of Canaan." (Exodus 33:18). The Hebrew word *Shalem* (which was the name of that city) means whole and is from the same root as *shalom* (peace). Jacob was injured from his night wrestling with the angel, who had wrenched Jacob's hip socket as dawn approached, but once he was renamed Israel, he arrived *shalem* (whole) and was able to find *shalom* (peace).

In one of her many brilliant sermons, Rabbi Sharon Brous said that: "the only way forward is through the truth." That's what Esther taught me in their life and her death. My only way forward towards the possibility of wholeness would entail confronting scary and excruciating truths.

But as miserable as I was that night, I had no idea that the real pain was yet to come.

Before the Biopsy

December 10, 2021

A couple weeks later, at my annual check-up, my doctor did a routine Pap smear, as women typically have every couple of years to test for cervical cancer. The procedure involves inserting a speculum into the vagina to open up the walls of the vagina, and then using a brush to take some cells from the cervix to test them for cancer. The doctor who conducted the procedure told me that I had a polyp that needed to be removed from my cervix.

"What is a polyp?" I asked.

She explained that a polyp is an extra piece of tissue that grows in your body. She said that it needed to be removed and biopsied to be sure that it wasn't cancerous. She said it was probably not cancerous, but it needed to be removed and checked, just in case. My doctor was a general practitioner, so she could remove the polyp herself but suggested that I call my gynecologist to schedule the polyp removal.

As soon as I finished my appointment and got to my car, I called my gynecologist to schedule an appointment to have the polyp removed. I didn't even wait to drive the fifteen-minutes it would take to get home before calling my gynecologist. I knew that until I heard the polyp was removed and I was told that it wasn't cancerous, I would be worried. So, I wanted the polyp removed as soon as possible. Unfortunately, though, the earliest appointment I could get with my gynecologist for the procedure was over a month away.

We were in month twenty-one of the pandemic, and the entire health care system was backed up as a result. My gynecologist had babies to deliver and other emergencies to handle, so the polyp removal wasn't the highest priority type of procedure to schedule. But I didn't want to live with this worry for over a month. Since my gynecologist wasn't available for a month and a half, I hoped to find another gynecologist who could see me sooner.

I didn't know how to find out which other gynecologists would be covered by my insurance, so I called my husband Tal and told him that I needed a list of the gynecologists covered by our health insurance. (Our health insurance is through his work, and he regularly deals with our insurance company. I didn't know how to gather this information, but I knew he could easily generate the list).

"Why?" he asked me.

"I just need the list. Please make it for me." I answered. He emailed me the list a few minutes later.

I didn't want to tell him why I needed the list of gynecologists. I figured there was no reason for him to worry about it. I knew that I would be worried, but it seemed kinder to spare him from worrying as well.

It's fair to say that my husband and I are both worriers. We come from long lines of professional Jewish worriers. In fact, if we didn't come from families of worriers, we probably would have never met. Worry led my grandparents to flee Poland and Russia several decades before the Holocaust to get away from religious persecution as they feared that things would get worse. On Tal's side, his parents had left Israel when he turned fourteen because his mom was worried about the prospect of him and his brothers going to war since military service is required of Israeli citizens who live in Israel past age fourteen. His mother was scared that he and his brothers and her husband would die in battle. His father, who had nearly died in battle during the Yom Kippur War, wanted to spare his sons what he went through. On both sides of our family, it's quite possible that worrying saved our lives. Worrying certainly brought us to this country. So, we're good at worrying. Tal and I are often up in the middle of the night worried about various concerns. If I could spare Tal a month and a half of worrying, then I was determined to do so.

That evening and several times over the next few days, Tal asked me why I needed a new gynecologist, but I refused to answer. "Woman stuff," I told him. "It's not your problem," and he stopped pressing me about it.

While I meant well by wanting to spare Tal suffering, this choice came at a cost. Although I spared him worry for days, I also created distance between us. He knew that I was being evasive to his questions. He could tell that I wasn't myself. I was agitated, but he didn't know why and therefore couldn't help me. By keeping this information to myself, I had shut myself off from him.

The day after the Pap smear, I started feeling pain in my cervix. I thought maybe I was just sore from the speculum used in the Pap smear, so I went to bed early. But the next day, rather than going away, the pain was gradually increasing. This pain further increased my worries. With the area hurting more and more, I was having trouble convincing myself that the polyp was probably nothing to worry about.

I called all the gynecologists on the several page long list that Tal had sent me of those covered by my insurance, and none of them had openings any sooner than my gynecologist did. The receptionists also made clear that if I made an appointment with any of them, it would mean that I was switching to them being my gynecologist permanently. I'd had the same gynecologist for eighteen years. She had been my gynecologist for both of my pregnancies. I didn't want to switch to a gynecologist I had never heard of permanently. I just wanted this polyp removed and biopsied as soon as possible, so that I could be relieved of worrying about the possibility of cervical or uterine cancer. All the gynecologists on the list didn't have openings for new patients in the coming weeks.

Another complicating factor was that we had a two-week vacation scheduled for a week and a half later. How could I enjoy the vacation with this on my mind? And I was in pain (which was getting worse by the day). We were going to visit friends of Tal's who I had never met in Lake Havasu. I didn't even know the names of these friends. I was in the shower when it occurred to me that perhaps I could ask his friend's wife if she had a gynecologist there and I could make an appointment to have the polyp removed while we were there, if it was covered by the insurance.

The only problem with this plan was that I couldn't figure out how to get any of this information without telling Tal why I needed it. I didn't know the name of the wife, her phone number, and whether the procedure would be covered by our insurance if we were out of town. Asking Tal for this info would raise a lot of questions.

I started asking Tal these questions: what were the names of the friends? Does our insurance cover procedures if you go out of state? He started asking me why again, and I had no choice this time but to tell him the truth.

I told him to close the door, so that the kids couldn't hear, and I explained to him what was going on. "I'm having a problem," I said, and I told him the whole story.

"Let me help you," he said.

He told me that our insurance doesn't cover non-emergency procedures outside of the state, but he assured me that he would get my gynecologist to remove the polyp before we leave. He told me that he would call every day to see if she had a cancellation, and he would explain the situation and bother them enough that they would surely see me.

Tal excels in practical matters, and he is especially gifted at being annoying enough to people on the phone to get them to comply with his requests. Being persistent and annoying is actually a big part of his job as a lawyer. He was on it, he assured me.

He was right. I told him on Saturday morning what had happened. Monday morning when the doctor's office opened, he called them, and when they said they had no openings, he called again and again, every few hours to see if any cancellations had occurred. Within a couple days, he had gotten me an appointment to have the polyp removed before we left. In that moment, Tal modelled for me a kind of dogged persistence and advocacy that would be required repeatedly in my healing journey.

"Why didn't you tell me what was going on?" He asked me. I told him I didn't want to worry him.

"You have to let me help you," he said.

I was impressed that he managed not to worry about it. He assured me that he didn't think it was cancer. He researched on the internet and found that polyps were common and usually benign, and he managed to get me the appointment for the polyp removal before we went on vacation.

This experience made me think of a story in the book of Genesis about the creation of humanity. After creating the first human, God said,

> *It is not good for the human to be alone. I will make for him a helper opposite him...So God caused the human to fall into a deep sleep and took the side of the human and closed up the flesh at that site.*[2]

God separated the first human into two people, male and female.

"It is not good for the human to be alone…" I've often puzzled about this verse. I am an introvert, and I enjoy being alone. In fact, I need time to myself to recharge my batteries. During the first twenty-one months of the pandemic, one of the hardest things for me was not having any alone time at all. With the kids doing school virtually from home and Tal and I working from home, quarantine was very hard for me – precisely because I needed time to be alone and couldn't have it.

But reflecting on this moment, I realize that the verse is true. While some alone time is nice, ultimately, it's not good for the human to be alone.

When I look back on it now, I realize that this was the first time of many times in this journey of sickness and healing, that my instinct was wrong. This was the first but not the only time that I kept my pain to myself – hoping to spare others from being bothered. It was the first of many times that I struggled with asking for help when I needed it. My instinct to keep my pain a secret didn't spare anyone any suffering. It just cut me off from the love of people who cared about me.

In this instance, Tal was right, and I was wrong. Actually, God was right, and I was wrong. "It is not good for the human to be alone." This verse encapsulates the essence of our faith.

The rest is commentary.

The Hardest Part

December 20, 2021

(date of procedure)

The doctor had told me that the polyp removal was supposed to be a minor procedure. I might feel some soreness or cramping the next day; perhaps a little bleeding, but the discomfort would be mild. The next day, I would feel fine.

At first, the day after the procedure, the pain was mild, but as the day wore on, the pain grew more and more intense. By evening, it was unbearable.

I went to urgent care. There, they gave me the strongest painkiller they had and tried to examine me, but the painkiller wasn't strong enough. I was in agony. The doctor at urgent care told me to go to the emergency room.

Tal drove me to the hospital. He dropped me off in front of the emergency room, so he could find parking. They brought me a wheelchair, and when I tried to sit down, the pain was blinding. I screamed out to Tal not to drive away, and he walked me into the emergency room.

It was a scary time to be in the emergency room. It was December 2021 during a time of surging Covid cases. We were afraid of getting Covid at the emergency room, but we had no choice. I couldn't go home in this much pain. Because of the surge in the pandemic, the emergency room was packed. They were handling the worst cases first. Since I could stand and walk, my case wasn't considered as critical as others. We stood there waiting for hours while I suffered in pain, from 11:00 pm until about 4:00 am, until they brought me to a room. In the room, we waited another hour until a nurse and later a doctor came to see me.

They gave me a painkiller which helped a little but not enough. They examined me and couldn't figure out why I was having such a reaction to what was supposed to be such a minor procedure. During the night, they gave me a pelvic ultrasound and many other tests but the imagining all came back normal. Although they didn't see anything unusual in any of the tests, I was in agony. I couldn't sit up. When I tried, the pain was so strong, I immediately lied back down.

My gynecologist came in the morning to see me. She had been a leading gynecologist for over twenty years. She had been my gynecologist through each of my pregnancies and delivered my daughter. She is well-revered, as a leader in her field. But in all her years of her practice, she had never seen anyone have this kind of reaction to a simple polyp removal. "I'm stumped," she said.

She prescribed painkillers and antibiotics in case there was an infection and sent me home that morning. She suggested that perhaps the antibiotics would help, and if not, we could order more tests and see a pain specialist.

Thankfully, a few days later, she told me that the polyp wasn't cancerous. I was relieved, but I was in so much pain and didn't know what to do.

In the months that followed, we tried many, many treatments that didn't work. The antibiotics didn't help. The painkillers didn't help much. No sign of abnormality appeared in any of the many, many images that were taken of my body. This was good news, and yet it wasn't good news. Without a cause, there was little hope for a cure.

For the next five months, my doctors and I pursued a series of medical theories that were entirely incorrect, and we eliminated each of these ideas when each corresponding treatment didn't work. The first theory was that the pain could have been caused by an infection, but since the antibiotic didn't help, then it wasn't an infection. The pain specialist then suggested that it could have been a nerve that was harmed by the polyp removal procedure, so I had three different nerve block procedures each separated by a few weeks. Since none of the nerve block procedures helped with the pain, we determined that it wasn't a nerve issue. Then I went to a specialist at UCLA who examined me and said that the pain seemed to be coming from the bladder area. So, I had seven weekly bladder procedures which didn't help, so we determined that it wasn't the bladder.

This process was a physical and emotional roller coaster for me. Each time that we came to a new theory and prospective treatment, I would hope that this was "the one" – the solution that would end the pain. If the next procedure was a few days away, I would tell myself, just endure the pain for a few more days and then you'll have the right procedure, and the pain will end. Then each time a procedure didn't help with pain, I was crestfallen and scrambling to figure out what to do next.

When I think about this time, a couple quotes stick out to me. The first was from my colleague, Rabbi Adam Kligfeld. He said, "Pain is a monster." He knew this monster first-hand. About a year before my medical problems, his bicycle seat broke, leading him to fall and break his shoulder. His recuperation involved lots of pain and took much longer than he expected. He shared with the congregation how that year was the worst year of his life. Indeed, only those who have endured extended periods of time of pain realize just how cruel the monster of pain can be.

The second quote that sticks out to me was also from a supportive colleague, Rabbi Jon Hanish, of Temple Kol Tikvah (which means "voice of hope" in Hebrew). When I told him about what I was going through, he said, "Not knowing is the hardest part." He explained that once there is a diagnosis, then the person can start to grapple with the prognosis, but until then, not knowing is the hardest part.

Rabbi Hanish's words reminded me of a story in Genesis – the story which marks the beginning of the spiritual journey which resulted in the Jewish people. In Genesis, God told Abram to leave his country, birthplace and father's house and go to "a land that I will show you."[3]

Ilana Grinblat

In this verse, God asks Abram to leave behind his home and everything he has known but doesn't even tell Abram where he is going. The place of departure for the journey is clear; the destination is not.

Rashi, a medieval French biblical commentator, noted the great sacrifices that were involved in this journey. He explained that relocating causes losses in terms of money, reputation, and family. Those sacrifices are increased when you don't even know where you're going – because then you have the added pressure of uncertainty. As Rashi noted:

> *God didn't reveal to Abraham the land immediately to make it more beloved in Abraham's eyes, and to give him a reward for each word.*

Rashi pointed out how as on this journey, God also didn't reveal in advance the destination when God asked Abraham to go on a three-day trip to sacrifice Isaac. Likewise, when God told Jonah to go to a city called Nineveh and tell the people there to repent, God didn't tell Jonah what to say when he got there. Apparently, when God sends people on trips, God is in the habit of leaving out key details of the itinerary. (Don't hire God as your travel agent!)

Yet, Rashi also noted that for every sacrifice that God asked of Abram, God promised rewards. Since the trip requires sacrifices of money, reputation and family, God promised Abraham that he will become "a great nation, and I will bless you, and make your name great, and you will be a blessing."[4] Rashi noted that as a reward for the journey, God added a letter from God's name to Abram's name – (adding the letter *hey* from God's name) making Abram's name Abraham.

This name-change represented the spiritual transformation within Abram because of the journey. The addition of a letter from God's name into Abraham's name suggests that he got closer to God on the trip and emerged a bit wiser.

God promised Abram that as a result of the journey, he will "be a blessing."[5] Rashi explained:

> *Until now, the blessings were in My (God's) hand. I blessed Adam and Noah, but from now, you will bless whoever you desire.*[6]

Before the trip, Abram was certainly blessed, but after the trip, he not only is blessed but becomes an agent of blessing. As a result of the arduous trek, Abraham emerged with greater power to bless others.

This teaching rings true for me not only about Abraham's spiritual quest, but also about the arduous journey of illness and healing. For the first five months after my annual check-up, grappling with the unknown was incredibly difficult. I didn't know why I was in pain, and therefore what to do to make the suffering stop.

Through the last two years, I had (and have) no idea when or if I would be healing and what healing would look like. Would I be back to normal – the way I was before the procedure – or would I have to deal with this pain for the rest of my life?

Since it was too painful for me to sit down for nine months, I couldn't drive a car or even be a passenger in a car. As I was essentially homebound and disabled for nine months, I wondered whether I would be homebound and disabled for the rest of my life. Would I ever drive again? Would I ever regain my independence, or would I permanently be reliant on others?

In addition to the burden of the pain was the added agony of not knowing. Right away, I had left behind the life with which I was familiar, and my future was suddenly unclear with no end in sight.

This reality is true for everyone who suffers from a serious illness or injury. No one can tell you what day you will be better or if you will be better or what better even looks like. Since each person's body reacts differently to treatment, there are no guarantees. No one has a crystal ball with which to predict the future. (Even God doesn't offer one!) When the present is filled with pain and suffering, all you want is the hope of a better future – but no one can tell you when or if that future will begin.

In reflecting on the journey of illness and healing, I appreciate Rashi's point out how difficult it is to not know one's destination, and I like the idea that God is trying to give us extra blessings when we are suffering.

Indeed, there are unique gifts that come through during times of great distress. The friendships that develop in the worst times of life are much deeper than the relationships that happen in the good times. All the closest friendships in my life were forged or deepened during the worst times of my life. Some of my closest friendships began the year that parents divorced when I was seventeen, and some of my dearest friendships began or were deepened in this past year of pain. During the worst times of my life, I couldn't pretend that I was okay and didn't need anyone. Somehow, the relationships that came during those times are the ones that last.

Likewise, there are crucial life-lessons that emerge from the ashes of loss and pain. This book is an attempt to articulate the lessons and blessings that come from nearly two years of suffering – which are often so hard to see as you're going through them.

One of my healers repeatedly told me that what's happening isn't happening "to me" but "for me." This idea reminded me of God's words to Abram when God told him to go on the journey – *lech lecha*.[7] These words mean either "go to yourself" or "go for yourself." The letter *lamed* in Hebrew means both "to" and "for." Both meanings are true of Abram's journey. He travelled "to" himself – discovering himself more deeply. He also went "for" himself. Although the journey involved sacrifices, it yielded blessings and rewards.

Whenever my healer tells me that what's happening to me isn't happening to me but for me, part of me revolts inside. This much pain and suffering isn't for me! Like the Rabbis my sufferings are not dear to me.

Still, the orientation of this happening "to me" is a passive one, in which I am the helpless victim. The view of this happening "for me" makes me search for the blessings along this excruciating path. It makes me look for what I am learning, how I am growing, and how I can become more of a blessing to others. This shift in outlook makes a big difference. It leads me to deeper understanding of myself, God, and others. As Anthony De Mello, an Indian Jesuit priest, said, "Nothing has changed except my perspective, and therefore everything has changed."

During those first days of agony, the pain was blinding. It was all I could see. But now that I look back, I realize that some of the lessons that emerged from those horrendous days was that Rabbi Kligfeld was right. Rabbi Hanish was right, my healer was right, and Rashi was right too. Pain is a monster. Not knowing is the hardest part. When pain is compounded by uncertainty, one can only hope for a better destination ahead – and maybe a few blessings and a little wisdom gained along the way.

In the Waiting Room

January 6, 2022

(date of procedure)

When I finished my first nerve block procedure, I was waiting for Tal to pick me up from the pain specialist doctor's office (since I couldn't drive myself home). I couldn't sit because of the pain, and the procedure had made my legs unsteady, so I was standing, holding myself against the chair in the waiting room.

A sweet lady started talking with me. She asked how I was feeling since she was going to have a similar procedure.

Although we had never met before, we talked in great depth in a way that you wouldn't normally talk with someone you didn't know. She shared how she had struggled with chronic pain for many years, essentially for her entire adult life. She explained how she avoids taking painkillers that could be addictive because she was concerned about getting dependent on them. She once had a procedure which helped her dramatically with the pain, and for a day she was entirely pain-free and filled with joy – dancing around the house as she put away the laundry. But then the pain had returned the next day. She shared how her sister who didn't have any pain tried to be supportive to her but couldn't really understand what she was going through.

I was struck by the depth that our conversation took immediately – as though we were suddenly close friends. I realized that just by standing in that room, I had entered a different dimension. Anyone in that room would only be there if they suffered from enduring pain.

Ilana Grinblat

Anyone in that room knew the monster of pain well. Therefore, there was an instant bond that didn't need time to grow. The connection was forged already from the shared experience of pain, suffering, and struggle.

I realized that I had switched worlds. For most of my life, thankfully, I've been quite healthy. I felt sick throughout my pregnancies, but this wasn't illness – just difficult pregnancies. Sure, I have had other short-term illness before – chicken pox, strep throat, even viral meningitis which landed me in the hospital. But each of these illnesses was short lived – one or several weeks. Never before had I entered the land of those who are struggling with pain in a long-term, possibly unending way.

Her statement about her sister particularly struck me. One of my brothers has struggled with chronic pain and health struggles for his entire adult life. Have I really understood him until now? Not really. I visit him when he's in the hospital, but I didn't truly understand the struggles he's endured, as I've never had experiences that are even remotely similar.

Now, that I am wrestling with the pain, depending on others for my transportation and care, and grappling with the prospect of some kind of disability of unknown duration or character, I do feel greater sympathy for him, as well as for anyone who is enduring chronic pain. Listening to this lady in the waiting room describe the struggles she has faced for many, many years was humbling. I know how difficult this has been for me for the past several months, I cannot truly fathom what it would mean or feel like to endure this kind of suffering as the basic reality of one's existence year in and year out.

This conversation made me think differently about one of the oddest parts of the Torah. One of the Torah portions in the book of Leviticus describes a strange, ancient affliction called *tzara'at*. This mysterious ailment could take many forms. This disease can turn skin white and scaly. Oddly, the affliction can also manifest in clothing or even a house as a form of mold or mildew.

The Torah portion called *Tazria/Metsora* (Delivery/The Leper) which is easily the oddest in the Torah recounts in graphic detail all the

What Pain Teaches Us

ways that this disease could manifest and the ways that bodily fluids could be leaking from various places in the body in an assortment of disgusting ways.

Based on this conversation and my new experience of prolonged illness, a couple parts of the Torah portion struck me in a different way. Firstly, I appreciate how this part of the Torah acknowledges that bodies are messy. They leak fluids, unpredictably, from various orifices at various times, without our permission or control. Bodies don't cooperate. And healing takes time. No one – not even a priest – can wave a magic wand and make the affliction stop. (If I could have waved a magic wand to make the pain go away, I would have done so right away!)

Even with all the progress of modern medicine and technology in the centuries since from the Torah portion until today, bodies remain a mystery. With all that we know, there's so much that we still don't know about the human body and how it functions or fails to work. Each person's case is particular to their own body. One size does not fit all. A treatment that helps one person may not work for someone else. Each person needs to be examined and treated with great care, creativity, and appreciation of the particularity of their needs and situation.

Indeed, the portion describes in detail how the priest would examine the sick person to determine whether they had the affliction of *tzara'at* or not. If the person did have *tzara'at*, the priest would declare the person *tameh, tameh* (impure, impure) and the person would "dwell apart, outside the camp" for as long as they were infected.[8]

Previously, I had always read this part as an effort to contain the contagious disease of *tzara'at*, but now this idea resonates with me differently. The Torah seems to understand that those who are suffering from a serious illness are living in a separate place than those who are well, and that those who are healthy often have trouble understanding what the ill are going through. Outside the camp, those with *tzara'at* could find companionship from fellow sufferers, just as the lady and I did in the waiting room at the pain specialist's office.

Ilana Grinblat

There's another moment in the story that is particularly poignant. God instructed Moses to tell the priest exactly what to do when examining the sick person to determine whether s/he is afflicted with *tzara'at*. God explained:

> *The priest shall see the affliction on the skin of his body, if the hair in the affected patch has turned white and the affection appears to be deeper than the skin of his body, it is* tzara'at. *When the person sees him, he shall pronounce him impure.*[9]

A commentator named Rabbi Y.Y. Trunek of Kutena noted the repetition in this verse. The text says that the priest should "see" the affliction and should also "see" him (the afflicted person). Didn't the priest already see him? Why is the word see repeated twice?

Rabbi Trunek explained that:

> *This verse contains a hint, that when you check a person, you should not only look at the person's shortcomings, also at the person's strengths... This is the meaning of "and the priest will see the affliction," and afterward, "the priest will see him,"— he will see all of him.*[10]

Rabbi Trunek understood the importance of two kinds of seeing – not only noticing a person's flaws but also seeing their strengths and the totality of their being. These two levels of vision seem particularly important in cases of long-term illness. To be a supportive family member, friend, community-member, caregiver, or clergy, we need to be able to recognize the anguish that the person is going through – not to minimize or deny it, but to see it fully. But we also need to see that no matter how grave the malady, that affliction does not define the person. We need to see the totality of who they are.

These two types of seeing don't need to take long. Even in brief conversations like the one I had at the waiting room, by listening to the stories of those who are struggling and sharing our own, we glimpse the depths of the soul of the person we encounter. We truly accept that person for the totality of their being – their struggles, courage, endurance, and strength.

Surprise

April 20, 2022

After nearly four and a half months of pain, three failed nerve block procedures, and six failed bladder installation procedures, I was beyond frustrated and exhausted from the pain. Then my son Jeremy came home from school with some symptoms – a runny nose and a fever. I gave him a Covid test which came back negative, so I didn't isolate him right away, figuring he just had a cold.

Jeremy gave me a hug that day (as he usually does). I told him, "I don't think you should hug me today." But it was too late.

The next morning, he tested positive for Covid, and the following day, I started having symptoms and the subsequent day, I tested positive for Covid.

Hannah was scared. After over two years of doing everything in her power to avoid getting Covid, the disease had invaded her house. I told Tal to take Hannah out of the house and go away for the weekend. He and Hannah went away to Big Bear for the weekend, and then I told them that they weren't coming back into the house until Jeremy and I had both tested negative for Covid and the house had been professionally cleaned and aerated for twenty-four hours.

After the weekend in Big Bear, Tal and Hannah moved to a hotel near Hannah's school. Jeremy and I were together in the house quarantining for two and half weeks. Jeremy sent emails to his teachers, letting them know that he had Covid, and would be absent for as long as it takes for him to heal and test negative.

As I reflect on those difficult weeks, a few moments stand out to me. One day during his quarantine, Jeremy received a text message from a classmate, saying that he heard that Jeremy had Covid and wanted to check how he was feeling and send him best wishes for healing. Jeremy was surprised by this text because it came from a classmate from his technical theater class. This boy was more an acquaintance than a friend – they'd only spoken a few times. Of all the people he knew, Jeremy never would have guessed that this boy would be the one who contacted him, and he was enormously grateful. When you are sick and feeling vulnerable, these kindnesses make all the difference in lifting your spirits.

The moment reminded me of an inspiring book by my colleague, Rabbi Steve Leder, called *More Beautiful than Before: How Suffering Transforms Us*. Rabbi Leder wrote:

> *One of the things I often tell people who are in the beginning stages of a painful ailment or crisis is that they are gratifyingly about to find out who their friends are, and disappointingly who they are not. A lot of people run away when trouble comes to someone they know. Maybe because they subconsciously fear that the affliction will somehow metastasize to them, or maybe they just don't know what to say or do to help. But in any case, there is no doubt that some people will disappoint you when you are in need and others will surprise you with their ability to show up.*[11]

Like Jeremy, I too was extremely grateful for the friends who came through for me during this time. Particularly, I was grateful for my friend Ari, who is a doctor. We were close friends throughout college and dated for a few years beginning the weekend before college graduation. Since then, I called each year on his birthday and sometimes on other occasions – maybe once or twice a year to catch up. But living in opposite ends of the country, with all the busyness of life, we had kept in touch in only sporadically over the years.

A couple months into this pain, at a stage when they couldn't figure out what was wrong with me, I called him. My purpose wasn't necessarily to get his medical advice. I just felt like talking to him. But when he asked me how I was doing, I couldn't help but tell him of the struggles I had been going through.

He talked to me for a long time, trying to brainstorm with me what could possibly be happening. He asked me to send him all the imaging that I had received from the two emergency rooms that I had been to, and he got on a zoom with me and showed me the imaging in detail. He explained to me which body parts were shown in the imaging and looked in detail at the records. He didn't see anything unusual in the imaging or in the blood work. He told me to get a pelvic MRI and several other tests which I did right away. Then he reviewed the imaging from the MRI and blood work when it came back. (Again, it looked normal.) He suggested possible medical explanations and then helped me evaluate whether each one was the true cause or not.

As I got sicker and sicker quarantining at home with Covid, Ari called every few days and checked up on me. My condition was getting dramatically worse day by day, which raised new and particularly difficult questions each day. During this time, Ari was one step ahead of me the whole way. It often felt like he was narrating to me the next chapter of the story before it happened – helping me work out the issues as they arose or were about to arise. For example, I was concerned that Jeremy would test negative and be ready to go back to school, but I would still have Covid and be unable to take care of myself at home. I talked through the dilemma with Ari – that Jeremy had already missed so much school that we didn't want him to struggle with completing his requirements for high school graduation, and yet I was unable to take care of myself. (Ari recommended keeping Jeremy home a few more days if need be.)

I shared with Ari the most terrifying moments during these weeks. The scariest moment for me of this time was when I was coughing and had trouble catching my breath. Jeremy asked me repeatedly, "Do I need to take you to the hospital?" but I couldn't answer him yes, and I couldn't answer him no – because I was desperately trying to stop coughing and catch my breath. Then thankfully, I caught my breath. Ari told me to tell Jeremy that if anything like that happens again to call 9-11 and have me taken to the hospital.

Ilana Grinblat

At the advice of another doctor friend, Tal bought me a device which monitors my oxygen level. I told Ari what my oxygen level was, and he told me how to know whether it was time to go to the hospital and told me about occupational therapy and the kinds of help that I may need going forward. I felt bad that I was needing so much help, but Ari assured me that I had a pass for life to ask him medical questions. I was and continue to be extremely grateful.

Ari's friendship reminded me of a teaching by Rabbi Moses ben Maimon, a rabbi and physician from twelfth century Spain, wrote that there are different kinds of friends. This rabbi (also known as Maimonides) liked to make lists of ascending levels on different topics – such as ten levels of charity. This list articulated three tiers of friendship – with the third level being the highest.

According to Maimonides, the lowest level of friendship is called "*chaver toelet* (friend for the sake of benefit)."[12] He explained this type of friendship as:

> *a utilitarian association which depends on reciprocal usefulness. Two people need each other. When this usefulness disappears, the friendship collapses. There was nothing else to sustain it.*[13]

An example of this type of friendship may be a co-worker that you work well with at a job or a classmate that you collaborate with on a project with whom you lose touch after that job or project is over. Maimonides noted that in this type of friendship, *butal dovar, botal ahavah* – when the "thing" (like the job or project that you collaborated on) ends, then the love (or friendship) ends as well.

The second, higher, level of friendship is called "*chaver hanachat*" (which means "friend for satisfaction." Maimonides explains this type of friendship:

> *This relationship is based on something more than practical usefulness. Here two people share joys and sorrows; they lighten each other's load; they are*

friends, easing each other, counseling, listening, supportive and caring. Joys are heightened when shared; suffering are more intense when alone. Here, we have a spiritual intertwining of two people, a state of love and devotion.[14]

While this kind of friendship is wonderful, Maimonides notes that there is a third, higher level of friendship: *chaver hama'alah* (a higher friend).

This is the ideal relationship because it reflects a joint dedication to a common cause, values, and goals. Both are committed not only to each other but to lofty objectives beyond themselves.[15]

In essence, this third, highest level of friendship combines the prior two levels – and both contains the mutual caring for one another of *chaver toelet* (a friend for benefit) and the joint project of *chaver hanachat* (a friend for satisfaction) – where the goal can be making this world a better place.

In real life, our friendships don't come with pre-assigned labels from Maimonides telling us what type of friend each person is or will be to us. Yet moments of crisis often reveal to us the nature of our friendships in both disappointing and encouraging ways.

When we are sick, we may discover, as Jeremy did, that what seemed to him like a *chaver toelet* (a friend for benefit) – was actually a *chaver hanachat* (a friend for satisfaction). With that text message, Jeremy discovered that someone he thought was just an acquaintance was actually a caring friend – more so even than who he thought were his closest friends.

During catastrophic times, we may discover (as I did) that someone who was a *chaver hama'alah* (a higher friend), the closest type of friend, wasn't just a *chaver hama'alah* for several years but is a *chaver hama'alah* for life. We may find someone you thought of as a friend is actually an angel, sent to rescue you from dis-ease and despair.

Thank God for friends in all their assorted, surprising, delicious flavors.

They Mean Well

April 23, 2022

(date of positive Covid test)

The two weeks that Jeremy and I spent quarantining at home were painful in so many ways. Physically, I was getting sicker and sicker. My symptoms started with a fever and then moved on to runny nose, and coughing, but the hardest part was difficulty breathing.

Due to the pelvic pain, I could not sit down, but due to the Covid, I no longer felt steady on my feet and could only walk with a walker that I borrowed which had last been used by my step-grandfather. Somehow, it was as though I had aged four decades within a matter of days.

Since I couldn't sit, I had Jeremy stack up encyclopedias on top of the table and place a tray on top of the stack, so that I could eat standing up while holding onto the walker. Sometimes, if I felt particularly unsteady, Jeremy would have to feed me so that I could hold onto the walker with both hands.

It was a complete reversal of our roles. Whereas, I had fed him as a child, he was now feeding me instead. Often the roles of parents and children reverse gradually over a period of many years. But this shift didn't take place over decades. It happened within a couple days. My body was so run down from the five months of pain, that when I got Covid (even though I was vaccinated and boosted), I wasn't strong enough to fight back adequately against the disease. In short, I was a wreck.

During these two weeks, I faced several conflicts which drained my strength further. The first problem was trying to get the drug Paxlovid which is used to treat Covid. This medicine only works if it is taken within the first five days of the onset of the illness. Once I tested positive for Covid, I spent the next five days trying and failing to obtain this medicine. To get this medicine at that time, a person needed to either be age fifty or older or have a pre-existing condition. I was forty-eight years old. I did have a pre-existing condition – the five months of pelvic pain due to the polyp removal, but that wasn't the kind of pre-existing condition that the doctors considered to prescribe Paxlovid. They were looking for conditions like AIDS, diabetes, heart problems, or other autoimmune disorders – conditions that people had for many years, not for only five months.

First, I went to urgent care and told them I had Covid and asked if I could get Paxlovid due to the pelvic pain that I had been suffering with for the last five months. After a long wait, they told me no. They told me to take Tylenol, and other cold medications for my symptoms and that I would be fine. I tried calling my doctor who gave me the same answer. Then I tried talking to a friend locally who is a doctor who also turned me down.

The doctors all told me that Paxlovid is only intended for high-risk patients, to keep them from having to go to the hospital, and I wasn't at high risk for ending up in the hospital. All the doctors told me to rest at home – that I would be just fine – but I knew that I was very far from fine.

At the same time, I had a conflict with my folks. As I was rapidly deteriorating, they were concerned about my condition and worried that Jeremy was left to take care of me alone, which was a big burden to put on a teenager. They wanted either Tal or themselves to come back into the house to take care of me. They explained that since Tal and they were in good health with no pre-existing problems, even if they got Covid, they would probably be fine. I refused. I didn't want to expose anyone to Covid on my account and take a chance that they might get seriously ill or even die.

When I think back on this time, there's one phrase that sticks out in my mind. It is a saying that Tal said to me repeatedly during this time. "They mean well." It was his way of acknowledging that even though I fervently disagreed with the doctors who wouldn't give me the medicine and with my folks, they meant well. The doctors genuinely didn't realize how sick I was, and they were trying to reserve the medicine for the most serious cases. My folks were also coming from a place of love. They were worried about me and my health (for good reason). They were also concerned about Jeremy, their grandson, and the burden that this situation was putting on him. Even though I passionately disagreed with the solutions that they were offering to this dilemma, I could acknowledge that they were coming from a place of caring. They meant well.

This idea echoes another teaching of Maimonides where he writes about judging each person favorably. He explained that if there is:

A person that you don't know, and you are not aware of whether that person is righteous or wicked, and you see that person doing an action or saying something, that could be interpreted as good but also interpreted as evil, interpret that action as good, and don't think badly about that person.[16]

He further noted that:

However, when a person is known to be righteous and is renowned for good deeds, but one sees him perform a deed that looks wicked from all vantage points and could be interpreted as a good deed only with great difficulty or in a farfetched manner, one is (still) obligated to interpret it positively, since there is the possibility of it being good. It is not allowed to suspect him and on this, it said, "Anyone who suspects the worth shall be punished."[17]

In this passage, Maimonides explained in great detail the idea that Tal summarized in just three words: "They mean well." When good people make decisions with which we disagree, we should judge them favorably, since they are just trying to do the best they can from their perspective.

Understanding that someone means well doesn't mean that you must agree with them or assent to their demand. When I look back at that time, I'm grateful that I found within myself a side that was more assertive that usual. I found a part of me that was a fighter – that wouldn't take no for an answer – that would do whatever it takes to protect herself and her family. That side of me (which I hadn't seen much before) didn't care what anyone else said or thought about the situation – but just did what she thought was right, whether anyone else agreed or not. An egg when boiled in hot water gets harder. So too, my will became stronger when facing a life and death situation.

Once I had stood my ground and asserted my decisions and boundaries, I let go of my frustration. I knew that although we had passionately disagreed, each of us had truly meant well.

After two and a half weeks at home, Jeremy tested negative for Covid, and I went to the hospital. Once the house was cleaned and aerated, Tal and Hannah moved back home (since I was no longer there). I never got Paxlovid, since when I entered the hospital, the first five days of Covid had passed, and Paxlovid doesn't work after the fifth day. But I received intravenous fluids, nutrition, and monitoring of my oxygen and blood pressure, and good care.

By keeping Tal and Hannah and my parents out of the house while Jeremy and I were positive, I prevented them from being exposed to the disease. As soon as I got to the hospital, Jeremy was no longer burdened with having to take care of me; the hospital staff was now charged with that task. So, my folks and I both got what we wanted. I avoided exposing anyone to the disease, and they got their goal of making sure that I was taken care of and that Jeremy was relieved of that task.

Once I was no longer contagious, my folks came to see me. We had a pleasant visit. Neither my folks nor I said a word about the conflict that had ensued between us. We judged each other favorably. Although we had passionately disagreed, each of us had truly meant well.

The Real Heroes

April 28, 2022

(date of hospitalization)

"Do I need to take you to the hospital?" Jeremy had asked me when I was quarantining with him at home with Covid and couldn't stop coughing. I couldn't answer him. I was too busy trying to catch my breath.

The answer to Jeremy's question came a couple days later when I had a video call with the doctor who told me the time had come to go to the Emergency Room. This time was during a surge in the pandemic so the wait in the emergency room was long. After many hours, they put me in a small holding room. It is a compliment to call it a room. It was more like a small box, and they told Tal that since I was contagious, he couldn't stay with me. I was in that room alone for forty hours.

I could barely walk with a walker. I would run out of breath on the few steps between the room and the bathroom which was just outside the door. Whenever I spoke on my cell phone, I had to stop to catch my breath. It was terrifying.

Thankfully, I had my iPad with me which had a meditation app on it. I decided that I was on a meditation retreat, which happened to be located in a hospital, and I did one meditation after another. This mindset helped me to reframe the time in a positive way, from just waiting to being on an educational program.

After forty hours, the attendant told me it would be another forty hours until a hospital room would become available. When I spoke to

Ilana Grinblat

the ER doctor, in addition to describing my Covid symptoms, I also told her about the five months of pelvic pain since the polyp removal – including the three nerve-block and seven bladder installation procedures that didn't help. She said, "If you are getting to the end of Western medicine's ability to solve this problem, try Eastern Medicine." She explained that UCLA Santa Monica has an East-West medical center which does both Eastern and Western medicine. I could either wait another forty hours for a room to become available at UCLA Westwood or I could be transferred by ambulance to UCLA Santa Monica where I could see the doctor from the East-West medical center. I decided to be transferred by ambulance to UCLA Santa Monica.

In the transfer process and throughout my stay in the hospital, I was struck by how many people were involved in helping each step of the way. There was a person in charge of transporting me down the hall in the stretcher. Then, there was someone else to ride with me in the back of the ambulance. I had fallen into this network of people each of whom were there to care for me as I fell apart. These are the real heroes that you don't even think about until the moment you need them.

Rabbi Jack Riemer wrote that the main lesson we should learn from the pandemic is to appreciate those who we might otherwise forget. He wrote:

If there is anything that we ought to learn from this ordeal that we have been through, I believe that it is our obligation, not only to honor the scientists and the epidemiologists and the leaders of government----important as they are- ---but that it is our task to honor the manual laborers, the people whom no one seems to pay any attention to---for they too played a vital and an indispensable role in getting us through this ordeal.

Every year, on the High Holidays, Rabbi Riemer calls up the synagogue's donors to be honored for their generosity. On this coming High Holidays, he plans to call up the janitorial staff of his synagogue

What Pain Teaches Us

to honor them for scrubbing the seats and cleaning the prayer books to keep the congregants safe. He will call on congregants to be grateful for all "unsung heroes" of the pandemic – "those people who cleaned and scrubbed the subways every night between one and five in the morning," or who "cleaned the operating rooms between every surgery" and "the truck drivers who bring the food to your supermarket," and the list goes on. I too feel incredibly grateful not only to my doctors and nurses but to all those who transported me from one place to another, as well as those who cleaned up my messes, and kept me company.

Once I arrived at UCLA Santa Monica, there was a nursing assistant (whose name I don't recall) who was especially kind. When I wanted to eat dinner outside on the patio near my room, I was told that I needed him to accompany me on the walk and during the meal. He sat with me and told me his life's story. He had been a literature professor in Mexico but one of his brothers had come to America and encouraged him to follow. Here he took a course on being a nurse's assistant and began working in the hospital. Although he loved being a literature professor, he enjoyed this work more because of the direct way that he was able to help people when they needed him most.

I shared with him the parallels in my story. I too enjoyed teaching at the university and found a different depth of work when working as a congregational rabbi and helping people when they lost a loved one or faced another crisis. As we talked, I realized that this was the first in-person conversation I had with someone that I didn't know in over two years due to the pandemic. During the pandemic isolation, I certainly had many conversations but all of them were with people I already knew – the rabbis in the community and family, and almost all of those conversations were by zoom or phone. I hadn't shared a meal with someone I didn't know in years. I didn't realize how much I had missed the simple act of sharing a meal and listening to each other's stories!

During my stay, I also called a friend who I hadn't spoken to in quite some time. I called to apologize to her for something that happened years ago, a way in which I hadn't been sufficiently compassionate and understanding of her. Somehow, coming close to my mortality inspired me to make amends.

In Judaism, the holiday of Yom Kippur (The Day of Repentance) is a day each year where tradition asks us to rehearse our death – by not eating, drinking, or having sex and wearing a white *kittel* (shroud) which is what is worn for one's burial. This rehearsal is intended to inspire us to repair our relationships and settle our unfinished business while we still can. Whereas Yom Kippur is a dress rehearsal for death, my hospital stay was the first time that I experienced the real version of this experience. As I came closer to death than ever before, I felt compelled to atone.

Another significant shift that happened during my time in the hospital is that I decided to stop watching the news. Prior to that, I had watched the news every day to keep abreast of what was happening in the world. But in the hospital, I felt too fragile to do so. When I was quarantining at home with Jeremy, I had watched a sad movie, and in the middle, I had started crying so much that I couldn't continue watching it. When in the hospital, I decided not to watch any television, except *The Daily Show with Trevor Noah* which covers the day's headlines in a comic way. In my delicate state, both physically and emotionally, I avoided any upsetting content.

This change reflects a teaching from the book of Deuteronomy, where the text states that one should "put judges and officers on all your gates to administer justice." This verse is the basis of establishing a justice system. Yet the Rabbi Isaiah son of Abraham Halevi Horowitz, a sixteenth-seventeenth century commentator notes that this verse can also refer to our seven sensory gates – our two eyes, two ears, two nostrils, and mouth.[18] Read in this way, this verse calls on us to carefully monitor our sensory gates to be sure that what comes in and out is only what is healthy for us.

Throughout the year plus of my recovery, I followed the instinct that I had in the hospital and monitored closely what came before my eyes. I found that the late-night comedians Trevor Noah and Stephen Colbert kept me sufficiently informed on the news with a dose of laughter. I stopped watching the cable news and other heavier programming and sought out comedy and light-hearted entertainment. Life was heavy enough as it was.

During my time in the hospital, I was grateful for the calls of family and friends. One call which particularly stands out to me which was from a work colleague. Throughout most of the time that I was in the hospital, I continued working (until my job's HR department expressly forbid me from doing so). I was the only rabbi on staff at the Board of Rabbis which served as a helpline. The questions from colleagues, community members, and all sorts of people flowed in constantly for me to answer. Responding to these queries gave me something to do to pass the time in the hospital, and I felt a responsibility that this support system continues operating without interruption.

"You have to stop and take care of yourself." Mary told me on the phone. "If there's one thing this awful pandemic is teaching us is that we can't work all the time."

I was struck by her words. Up until that point, the pandemic had taught me precisely the opposite lesson. I had worked all the time – supporting my 222 colleagues and many community-members of all faiths through the three-year-long emergency.

It took me several months before I took Mary's words to heart and followed her advice. Two months after that phone call, I went on medical leave for a month, and a couple months later I resigned my position at the Board of Rabbis to focus on my health.

One of the blessings of my six and a half years at the Board of Rabbis was the way that it deepened my relationships with my colleagues. They were very supportive during my illness – reaching out with calls and emails. Once I was no longer contagious and in isolation, one of my colleagues, Rabbi Ahud Sela came to visit me at the hospital. He held my hand and said the prayer for my healing. I was receiving an IV of fluids and vitamins on my left arm, and he was holding my right hand during the prayer. So, I was simultaneously receiving physical and spiritual healing.

I am grateful for the heroes of all kinds who had cared for me during my week in the hospital and picked me up when I fell apart.

A Different Theory

May 3, 2022

While in the hospital, I met with Dr. Shubov of the East-West Medical Center. I shared with him the story of the five months of pelvic pain that I had been through thus far. I told him about the various treatments that we had tried which had failed. I explained that at first, they thought it was a nerve, so we tried three different nerve block procedures. Since they didn't help with the pain, the doctors concluded that it wasn't a nerve. Then, a doctor thought it was the bladder, so we tried seven bladder installation procedures, but since those didn't alleviate the pain, the problem wasn't the bladder.

"Can I share a different theory with you?" Dr. Shubov asked.

"Please." I replied.

He suggested that due to the pain of the polyp removal procedure, all the muscles in the lower half of my body tensed up as a protective mechanism and couldn't release. He explained while imaging shows a great deal, what doesn't appear on imaging is the condition of the muscles. He said that when most doctors see that no problems appear on the imaging, they stop thinking. They don't remember that muscles don't appear on the imaging, and that the worst type of pain is muscle pain. (He explained that childbirth is also a type of muscle pain.)

Dr. Shubov gave me shots into the muscles which helped. He told me to find a medically trained/certified massage therapist to work with me weekly on loosening up the muscles. Tal called a nearby massage place and asked if they had a medically certified masseuse. They had one, and we made the first available appointment after I was to leave the hospital.

In Dr. Shubov's explanation, I was struck by the idea that what was unseen – the muscles -- were more powerful (or painful) than what could be seen on the imaging. Indeed, the whole premise of Judaism is that the unseen – God – is more powerful that what we can see.

I was also struck by the idea that my muscles' instinct was to tense up to protect me from pain, but that instinct only caused me more suffering. In the coming months, in muscle massage, I would have to accept more pain which would lead to healing.

What happened to me physically is often true emotionally and spiritually. How often our efforts to protect ourselves from emotional pain only backfire and cause more pain. I have seen this pattern again and again. When we're in crisis, we close up emotionally. We think this will keep us from pain, but instead, it just causes us more isolation and suffering. That instinct had kept me from telling loved ones and community about my illness to spare from worry, but this just created more isolation and suffering. Telling people what was happening with me was painful, but it led to having more support for my healing.

This is true not only regarding illness but in other situations too. Shortly after Dr. Shubov offered his theory, I learned that two of my friends' sons were in a conflict where each boy felt the other boy was bullying him. I offered to mediate a conversation between the two sets of parents. One parent refused. I understood why. She was upset and angry about what her son was suffering and wanted to protect herself from an upsetting conversation with the other parent. Yet, I wonder whether that painful conversation could have led to reconciliation.

Dr. Shubov's theory saved my life by offering a path forward out of pain – one that has been proving successful, unlike all the other previous theories. It also taught me an important truth which applies not only to pelvic muscles but also to muscles like the heart and spirit. It taught me to be wary of our instinct to close up and protect ourselves from pain, which only causes more pain, and to accept the kind of pain which offers a chance at healing and hope. I am eternally grateful for this theory and for this truth.

The Decision:
A Mother's Day Reflection

Mother's Day: May 8, 2022

When I was quarantining at home with Jeremy, getting sicker and sicker with Covid, another level of drama was taking place. Jeremy had to decide where to go to college. The timing couldn't have been worse – as both Jeremy and I were so ill – but a deadline is a deadline. A choice had to be made, whether we were sick or not.

Jeremy had narrowed his decision down to two colleges. Both schools were California State Universities. We had visited both colleges and learned all that we could about the schools and the programs in film and theater production he was considering. Both were wonderful options.

In the days leading up to the deadline, Jeremy debated back and forth in his head, weighing the pros and cons. In the meantime, I had made the decision in my mind of which school I preferred for Jeremy. It had one of the highest ranked and best film schools in the nation and was close to home. My husband Tal had also determined which school he felt was best for Jeremy because the beautiful campus reminded him of the wonderful experience he had in college. Tal and I had come to opposite conclusions about which university would offer the best experience for Jeremy, but we both agreed that it should be Jeremy's decision.

Ilana Grinblat

Unfortunately, since Jeremy and I both came down with Covid a few days before the deadline for this decision, we were quarantining at home while Tal and Hannah spent ten days at a hotel to stay safe. This situation left me with a strange challenge – trying to help Jeremy make this decision without pressuring him to reach the decision I had reached.

I tried everything – listening as Jeremy shared his thoughts, helping him make pros and cons lists, but nothing worked. In the Talmud, when two rabbis extensively debate an issue and can't reach a decision, this is called *Teyku*. Jeremy had reached *Teyku* in his own mind. For him, the two schools were tied in the race.

I explained to Jeremy the Yiddish saying which says that 'you can't dance at two weddings with one *tuchus* (butt).' He couldn't attend both colleges next fall.

I tried an experiment with Jeremy. I walked into the room and said, Jeremy, I've decided that you will go to _____ for school (filling in the name of the school). I then left the room and came back in and said the same sentence inserting the name of the other school. I asked Jeremy to notice how he felt each time. He said that he felt more excited in reaction to one of these statements than the other. Having discovered that he felt more joy about one of the schools, he finally made his decision. One school had won the race in Jeremy's mind by a hair, but it wasn't the school I preferred for him.

This experience was new for both of us. Jeremy had never made a decision like this before. I had never accepted him making a choice with which I disagreed. In this one moment, he became an adult, and I became the mom of an adult.

Ironically, while Jeremy was making a decision with which I disagreed, I was making a decision with which my parents disagreed. Out of love, knowing how sick Jeremy and I were, my stepmom and dad were insisting that either Tal or one of them come into our home to take care of me. Out of love, I refused to let them come into the house because I didn't want to endanger them by exposing them to Covid. As I was struggling as a parent to accept Jeremy's right as an

What Pain Teaches Us

adult to make a decision with which I disagreed, my parents were facing the same challenge – to accept my choice which they opposed.

There is a Hebrew phrase for the struggle of raising children – *Tza'ar gidul banim*. There should be a specific word for the pain of accepting the decision of an adult child with whom you disagree. My folks and I were experiencing that specific type of anguish.

At the same time, the country was also deadlocked in a fierce, excruciating debate. A draft of a Supreme Court ruling had been leaked which showed that the court intended to overturn Roe vs. Wade and take away a woman's right to choose whether to have an abortion or not. The country was facing the same kind of question my folks and I was facing: Would we accept the right of an adult to make their own decisions – regardless of whether we agree.

As we watched the coverage on television, Jeremy saw how upset I was about the leaked ruling. "You want babies to be killed?" he asked, puzzled.

"No," I replied, "but I want women to have the right to make their own decisions about their bodies, regardless of whether I agree with those decisions."

As my Covid worsened, I ended up in the emergency room with trouble breathing. From my hospital bed, I read a reflection by one of my former students, Rabbi Myra Meskin, in honor of Mother's Day which explored the biblical story of Pharaoh's daughter who rescued baby Moses when he was floating in a basket down the river and raised him as her son.

In the Torah, she is called Pharaoh's daughter, whereas in a rabbinic legend she is called Batya, meaning "daughter of God."[19] According to this *midrash* (rabbinic story), since Pharaoh's daughter showed mercy to baby Moses and raised him as her son, even though he was not her biological child, God decided that she had merited to be called Batya, the daughter of God.

Rabbi Meskin noted that the act of taking compassion on Moses was an explicit act of rebellion against her father, Pharaoh, because it was her father who had decreed that the Israelite male babies be killed.

Ilana Grinblat

By saving baby Moses' life, Batya explicitly disobeyed her father's order that all Hebrew babies be killed.

Rabbi Meskin wrote:

> *By willingly ignoring and undermining her father's decree by taking Moses in, she extracts herself from her father's domain.*[20]

How poignant and ironic that for Batya, the moment she defied her parent was the moment she became a parent herself!

Reading Rabbi Meskin's reflection made me feel so proud that my parents chose to name me after Batya, as my Hebrew name is *Ilana Batya*. I now felt a new connection with my namesake.

As was true for Batya in the Torah, making a choice in opposition to a parent's wishes can be a defining moment in life – the moment when one truly becomes an adult. When Jeremy made the college decision I disagreed with, he became an adult. When I accepted his choice, I became the parent of an adult. At that moment, he left my domain and entered God's domain – where he follows his own path rather than mine.

Ironically, several weeks later, Jeremy changed his mind and decided to go to the school I preferred for him. However, his change of mind had nothing to do with my opinion of either school, but rather had to do with more information he had learned about each of the programs. He decided to stay locally to continue working with the contacts he made over the spring and summer in the film industry. He wanted to stay in Los Angeles, not because of its closeness to home, but because of the proximity to the movie industry.

Even though he changed his mind about schools, the moment of his reaching adulthood wasn't reversed. *He* had changed his mind on his own – following his own best judgement, not that of either of his parents or his relatives. Although he changed his decision, he stayed in his own domain.

While I was in the hospital, Mother's Day came. The night before, the doctors had determined that I was no longer contagious, and as a result my children and my parents visited me on Mother's Day.

This Mother's Day was certainly unlike any I'd ever experienced. Before the pandemic, my husband, children, and I would typically go to a decadent Mother's Day brunch buffet with Tal's side of the family– and then go to a delicious dinner with my stepmother and grandmother, father, and my siblings. My mother-in-law and stepmother would certainly have preferred to have those meals as usual, but they cancelled them due to my hospitalization. Still, I was grateful to see my children and my folks at the hospital on Mother's Day.

My mother-in-law, my stepmom, and I reluctantly accepted that this Mother's Day we'd do what was best for our adult children at this painful moment – even though it wasn't what we wanted. After all, that's what motherhood is all about.

The Megaphone

May 10, 2022

(date of discharge from hospital)

While I was in the hospital, my dear friend Deborah let the Temple Beth Am community know about my condition. A group within the synagogue called the library minyan sent an email out with a sign-up sheet for people to bring my family meals when I returned home.

For two weeks, members of the library minyan brought dinners to our house every night. One person brought me fresh picked strawberries from the Farmer's Market. For the Sabbath, one person made a home-baked *challah* (braided bread); another person brought a made a main course, another brought over soup, and yet another brought home-made dessert. My family and I have never eaten so well in my life as we did for those weeks!

I was incredibly touched by the kindness of all these people. I found it especially moving because we hadn't been to Temple Beth Am in years. We had attended services the library minyan every week for over ten years. However, due to the pandemic, we had been cautious and avoiding in-person gathering so we hadn't been to that synagogue in over two years, but still, one email went out and two weeks of meals arrived.

Each time someone brought a meal, they would talk with me. Along with the food, they brought their best wishes, prayers, and advice. Of these visits, one particularly stood out to me. It was from a congregant named Susan Mishler who was a medical professional and had faced

Ilana Grinblat

complicated health challenges. "Use a megaphone," she said. She explained that I should tell everyone I know about my medical problem "because you never know who may know someone who knows someone who can help."

This advice struck me because I had instinctively done precisely the opposite. At that point, I had been in pain for five months and had told virtually no one other than our immediate family, Ari, and my employer. I had simply been powering through as best I could, only telling people on a need-to-know basis —when I couldn't get away with not telling them. I'd had two hospital stays in the five months prior to my week in the hospital, but since those previous two visits were short, we kept them to ourselves. Only this time, since I was in the hospital for a week, did word get out more broadly.

I thought of King Solomon's poem in the book of Ecclesiastes:

> *There is a time for everything,*
> *and a season for every activity under the heavens:*
> *a time to be born and a time to die,*
> *a time to plant and a time to uproot,*
> *a time to kill and a time to heal,*
> *a time to tear down and a time to build,*
> *a time to weep and a time to laugh,*
> *a time to mourn and a time to dance,*
> *a time to scatter stones and a time to gather them,*
> *a time to embrace and a time to refrain from embracing,*
> *a time to search and a time to give up,*
> *a time to keep and a time to throw away,*
> *a time to tear and a time to mend,*
> *a time to be silent and a time to speak…*

For five months, I had tried silence – which hadn't worked well. Now, it was "a time to speak."

Susan also gave me another piece of advice. She suggested that every time I speak to a doctor, I should ask them: 'What would you do if this was you, or your daughter or your wife?'

When retelling the story of Passover, the Passover Haggadah states that 'in each generation, each person should see themselves as if they had come out of Egypt.' We're not simply supposed to retell the story, we are supposed to envision ourselves as if we personally were in the story.

Likewise, this advice suggested that I prompt the doctors to envision themselves as if they were in my shoes – or their wife, or their daughter – and ask then point blank what they would do. Her advice modelled to me the type of persistence and advocacy for myself that would be needed to find the answers to get out of the prison of pain. In the coming months, I would ask many such pointed questions to try to get more information and follow every lead that might help.

Overall, these two weeks of meals showed me the power of community. The idea of community was not new to me. I had lived my entire life as part of close-knit Jewish community. Growing up, our home was four doors down and across the street from the synagogue. The synagogue was an extension of our home; the synagogue members were our extended family. I remember once there was a bomb threat to the synagogue, and services moved to our home instead.

I had grown up immersed in community and had worked in the Jewish community for twenty years, yet these two weeks of feeling cared for brought home to me the power of community in a deeper way. The synagogue may look like a building which holds religious services, but really that's just a facade for a network of people who are committed to be there for and care for one another, week after week, year after year. No less than the hospital workers, these community-members are there to pick each other up when they fall.

Throughout these two weeks, the kids were blown away by the delicious food that kept coming every day. I was grateful that they saw this powerful display of caring. They may have wondered why we went to services every week for all those years. Now, they could witness first-hand the power of community to sustain you and lift your spirits when in crisis.

Soon after, I received another potent demonstration of the power of community – through my work at the Board of Rabbis (which is a program of the Jewish Federation of Greater Los Angeles). I received an email from a colleague at the Federation that a lay leader had happened to meet a rabbi named Steve at the intensive care unit of Cedars-Sinai hospital. The rabbi and his wife who lived in Mexico had been visiting their children for Passover when his wife had a medical emergency which landed her in the hospital. Their children lived in a small apartment in the Valley (which is not close to this hospital). So, the rabbi was spending $200 a day between staying at an Air B&B and taking Ubers to and from the hospital. When I received this email, she had been in the hospital for two months, and the daily expenses were not sustainable.

My work at the Board of Rabbis entailed supporting the rabbis of Los Angeles, so since he was a rabbi, Andrew had reached out to me to assist Rabbi Steve. I asked my dad and stepmom Melissa for suggestions. On Saturday, at the library minyan service, Melissa made an announcement at services about the situation, asking for ideas of where he could stay.

Traditionally observant Jews don't use computers on the Sabbath until three stars appear in the sky on Saturday night. Indeed, as soon as three stars appeared in the sky on Saturday night, I began receiving emails from congregants offering places for the rabbi to stay. One congregant lived only a block from the hospital, so I put the rabbi in touch, and he stayed there. Then another congregant who was going on vacation offered to help, so he stayed there for two weeks. I lent the rabbi my car since I wasn't well enough to drive and when we went on vacation, he stayed at our home for a week.

Then the stepdaughter of a colleague went on a trip to Paris for a few months, so the rabbi stayed at her place. Through the generosity of these families, I was able to arrange for the rabbis housing and transportation for three months until sadly his wife died in the hospital. Throughout this time, Rabbi Steve and I talked and supported one another through these months of my medical crisis and that of his wife. I prayed for his wife, and he prayed for me. Even as we were each falling apart, we held each other up.

Like me, the rabbi hadn't reached out to the Jewish community for help. Still, the help found him. The networks of the Jewish Federation of Greater Los Angeles, the Board of Rabbis of Southern California, and Temple Beth Am were immediately activated and came through in spades.

When the rabbi expressed his thanks to me, I told him about something that happened to me many years before. When I was in college, I spent two semesters abroad, one in rural Ecuador, volunteering in a one-room schoolhouse, and one in Ghana studying West African culture. These semesters were both in the fall – one year apart. Before I went to Ecuador, my father agreed that I could go on one condition. I had to find a Jewish family to stay with for the High Holidays.

"How am I supposed to find a Jewish family in Ecuador?" I asked my father.

"Call the American Embassy of Ecuador and ask if they knew a Jewish family you can stay with for the High Holidays," he replied.

This idea sounded ludicrous to me. I didn't think it would work, but my father is persistent. When he wants me to do something, he repeats his request every day until I finally comply – just so that he'll stop bugging me about it. So, I called the embassy and asked. The person who answered the phone knew someone Jewish who agreed to host me.

They were a lovely family whose children had grown up. I stayed in their daughter's room and attended the High Holiday services at the synagogue in Quito, the capital of Ecuador, and ate the holiday meals with them at their home. After the holidays, they became my support network for the semester. A month later, while living in the rural village, I came down with strep throat, and I travelled back to their home and stayed with them. They helped me get the medicine that I needed and hosted me until I recovered and returned to the village.

I was very grateful and surprised by their generosity. They didn't know me or anyone in my family. All they knew is that I was Jewish and needed a place to stay, and that's all they needed to know – and they were there for me. Although I had grown up with Jewish community, this experience in Ecuador taught me the value of Jewish community in a new way. I was halfway around the world, but I wasn't alone. I was part of a people – a worldwide support network of people who cared for one another in good times and bad.

A year later before I went to Ghana, my dad made the same condition for approving and paying for my semester abroad: I needed to find a place to observe the High Holidays. This time, when I called the embassy, they directed me to an Israeli company that was working on improving irrigation in Ghana. There were approximately a hundred employees of this company. A family graciously agreed to host me for the holidays. They didn't have a synagogue, but they gathered for services, and I ate holiday meals with this host family. My experience of the hospitality of the family and community in Ecuador wasn't a fluke. It was replicated precisely during my semester in Ghana.

When Rabbi Steve expressed his thanks for my assistance during his wife's hospital stay, I told him about the families in Ecuador and Ghana. I explained that I wasn't doing anything extraordinary. I was only doing what I had learned from them about how Jews care for one another wherever we find ourselves throughout the world. I hadn't given the families in Ecuador or Ghana anything for the generosity they showed me. Yet, I was able to pay their kindness forward some nearly thirty years later for Rabbi Steve. I demonstrated what I had learned from them, from my dad, and from the library minyan of Temple Beth Am about the value of community especially when you're far from home or facing illness. When we're most vulnerable, the generosity and kindness of community-members remind us that we're not alone.

What Pain Teaches Us

On the first day of the High Holidays (on Rosh Hashanah, the Jewish New Year), the Torah reading is from the book of Genesis. The text doesn't specifically mention the holiday, so the rabbis could have chosen any story from the entire Torah to read on this holiday.

The chapter that they chose (Genesis chapter 21) retells the story of Abraham following Sarah's advice to send away his maidservant Hagar and their son Ishmael into the desert with little food and water. It's not a cheery story. It wouldn't have been my first choice of what to read on this festive day. Actually, it's one of the most disturbing stories in the Torah so it would have been at the bottom of my list of choices for readings.

Yet, maybe that's because I'm focused on the wrong characters – Abraham and Sarah – what were they thinking?! Perhaps the rabbis were focused on Hagar's story. While in the desert, Hagar ran out of food and water. In despair, she put her infant son Ishmael down a bowshot distance away to avoid seeing him die. Then she saw a well of water in front of her.

Significantly, the text doesn't say that a well of water appeared. In the Torah, often things magically appear just in the nick of time (including a talking donkey or a splitting sea). But in this case, the Torah doesn't say that a well of water appeared. Instead, the Torah states:

> *Then God opened her eyes and she saw a well of water. She went and filled the skin with water and let the boy drink.*[21]

The miracle that Hagar experienced was that of recognizing something that she didn't see before. In her despair, she hadn't seen the well of water, but then God opened her eyes so she could see it.

Likewise, for me the power of community has been there right in front of me throughout my life, but at certain moments, my eyes were opened to see that power in a different way than before. The family in

Ecuador and then the one in Ghana opened my eyes to the power of community when I was far from home

Nearly thirty years later, the library minyan members of Temple Beth Am opened my eyes to the power of community to uplift my spirits when I was gravely ill. The Jewish Federation, the Board of Rabbis, and the library minyan opened the eyes of Rabbi Steve from Mexico's eyes to the power of community. For both Rabbi Steve and I, we had devoted our careers to serving community – and yet, only at the lowest moments in our lives were our eyes opened to the power of community in a new way. Like Hagar's well, the community gave us the strength to move forward when our hopes were at the lowest point.

At the library minyan, on the first Sabbath after I left the hospital, I said a special blessing called Birkat Hagomel – which is traditionally said upon surviving a life-threatening situation. The words of the prayer are:

>*Baruch ata Adonai eloheinu melech ha'olam hagomel l'chayavim tovot shegemalani kol tuv.* (Blessed are You, God, our God, sovereign of the world, who bestows on the undeserving goodness, who has bestowed upon me goodness.)

This blessing too deserves to be said with a megaphone.

The Blanket

May 12, 2022

Soon after I got out of the hospital, I received a package in the mail. The package contained a blanket – the softest one I've ever felt. The green blanket had encouraging words written on it in white – "Warm hugs, prayer, positive thoughts, strength," etc.

I was incredibly moved and surprised by this unexpected gift. The present had come from a work colleague of my husband and his wife –and Kathy Bauducco.

I was particularly surprised because I don't know them very well. I see them every year at the firm holiday party (which due to the Covid pandemic hadn't occurred for several years, so I hadn't seen them in years). They are always friendly with me and my husband – but he works in a different department at the firm than my husband, so he is not one of the colleagues that Tal works with most closely. As a result, I was floored and flabbergasted that Paul and Kathy got me such a thoughtful gift. I didn't even realize that word had gotten out to Tal's co-workers that I had been sick.

We immediately emailed them to thank them, and Paul's response was: "No thanks necessary." He explained that he remembered "a very dark day" when his son was in the hospital at UCLA Medical Center with a broken neck and Tal showed up to support them. Fortunately, Kathy and Paul's son walked out of the hospital four days later after emergency spinal surgery and recovered.

Ilana Grinblat

This response was so moving to me. I don't know how many years ago this visit took place, but the visit meant so much to Paul and Kathy that all these years later, they gave me this blanket. When Tal left the hospital room that day, he probably thought that the visit was over, but it wasn't.

All these years later, the visit endured and transformed into another act of kindness -- into a blanket. That blanket was with me throughout my illness. I slept under it every night. Each day for my treatment program, I was supposed to do several hours daily of a relaxation audio program that Dr. David Wise created. I found it difficult to keep focus and to do this program while in pain. Every time I did the relaxation exercises, I was under that soft blanket, covered with the healing words and best wishes of our friends on my skin.

Somehow, the kindness we do last much longer than we think. I remember my step-grandmother, Sandra Patack, would spend hours cooking to make elaborate Shabbat dinners for our family. Although she loved cooking, she would often complain that she would spend so many hours creating food that only took a few minutes to eat. Yet, I suspect that those dinners lasted a lot longer than she thought – much longer than a few minutes.

Bubby (grandma) Sandra died eight years ago. But her daughter, my stepmother Melissa and her granddaughter, my sister Mira, still make her *challah*, desert and other recipes for Shabbat (the Sabbath). Whenever they do, they always say that this was *Bubby*'s recipe, and we all remember and miss her – including Jeremy and Hannah, her great-grandchildren. Those meals fostered – and still foster the love of a family. They endure to this day and Mira will surely teach those recipes to her children and grandchildren and share with them her memories of Bubby. So, those meals didn't end after a few minutes of eating – they are lasting for generations.

Shortly after receiving the blanket, I spoke about the blanket in a sermon for Temple Har Shalom in Idyllwild, where I serve as a rabbi. That week's Torah portion was Balak, a Torah portion from the book of Numbers, which tells a colorful story about a wizard named Balaam who was hired by a king named Balak to curse the Israelites, who Balak perceived as a threat. Balak took Balaam to a mountain below which the Israelites were encamped and asked him to curse them. But when the moment came, Balaam spontaneously blessed them instead, saying:

> Ma Tovu Ohalechah Yaakov, Mishkenotechah Yisrael *(How good are your tents, Jacob, your dwelling places, Israel.)*[22]

This blessing became the words that Jews traditional recite whenever they enter a sanctuary. It is a song that is sung at the beginning of nearly every Jewish service around the world throughout the centuries. Its words are affixed on the outside of many synagogues as well.

I suspect that when Balaam said those words on the hilltop, he thought that the blessing was done as soon as he closed his mouth. He would never have suspected that thousands of years later, his words would be said throughout the world in places he'd never even heard of.

Likewise, when I went on a trip to Alaska with my children's Jewish Scouts troop, one of the troop leaders Dr. Sheila Keiter (who teaches Jewish studies at a Modern Orthodox High School in Los Angeles), was studying Talmud on a picnic table near a river. As I watched her, I thought about the rabbis from ancient Babylonia whose teachings were contained in the Talmud (which was edited in the sixth century C.E). I imagined that they would be so flattered to know that over 1500 years after they spoke their teachings, they were being studied over 9000 miles away from where they lived in a place they probably never heard of and surely had never visited.

I also remember that only a couple weeks into the Covid pandemic, I attended a zoom *bar mitzvah* (coming of age ritual). During this service – as is typically done in Shabbat (Sabbath) morning services -- psalm 145 which is called the *Ashrei* (which means happy) was sung. The song was recited by a young boy, the cousin of the *bar mitzvah* boy. According to tradition, this psalm was composed by King David, who reigned from 1040-970 B.C.E.

Ilana Grinblat

Watching the boy sing the psalm, I thought how astonished King David would have been when he wrote this song if he knew that over 3000 years later, there would be a plague that would keep people from being able to be in the same room but by then people would have invented a technology with which they could see one another even if they weren't in the same place – and even then, in that new technology, kids would still be singing his song.

At those moments, you glimpse the marvel of the human spirit. Our teachings, our creations (like our yummy treats), last far longer than we think.

Ian Maclaren, a nineteenth-century minister in Scotland, famously said, "Be kind, for everyone you meet is fighting a hard battle." I would add to those words – be kind because your kindnesses outlast your expectations. Actually, your kindnesses even outlast you.

A visit to a sick or grieving friend doesn't end when you walk out of the room. It lives on and transformed into a new creation. It may come back to you, or it can be paid forward in an entirely form to someone you have never met and will never meet, who then transforms it into another kindness to someone else and the chain goes on and on. The *challah* or blond brownies you make today may be enjoyed by your great-grandchildren and theirs (or someone else's great grandchildren). Thousands of years later, in a land you've never visited or even heard of, the Torah of your life can continue and touch someone's heart.

And just maybe, a hospital visit can just come back to your home as a blanket that warms your heart when you need it most.

The Turning Point

June 9, 2022

After returning home from the hospital, in one of my follow up appointments with Dr. Shubov, he recommended that I read a book called *A Headache in the Pelvis* by Dr. David Wise. I promptly checked the book out from the library, laid down on a blanket in the grass in my backyard and started to read.

As I read, I learned that Dr. Wise had suffered from pelvic pain and couldn't sit down for twenty years. He searched for cures for many years to no avail, and he eventually invented a series of devices to press on various trigger points in the body to release the pain. As I read, I was captivated. For the first time in the five months that I had been in pain, someone was describing precisely the problem that I was having and offering solutions to it.

After a few chapters, I started looking online for more information about Dr. Wise and discovered that he conducts weekend workshops once a month teaching his techniques to those suffering with pelvic pain. The next workshop was one week away.

Immediately, I was on a mission to get myself to that workshop which was no small feat. The workshop was to convene in in a small town called Petaluma in Northern California, about eight hours by car from where I live. It is not near an airport, and there's no train to get there. How was I going to get there without being able to sit down? Who would take me to the workshop since I couldn't drive?

First, I had to convince Tal since the workshop was expensive and not covered by insurance. Then, I had to figure out the logistics of travel and hotel. I had to fill out a lot of paperwork for the workshop and get a special prescription from my doctor – all of which had to be done within a few days.

But I was determined. I was going.

I remembered a piece of advice that Ari had given me in our phone conversations before I went to the hospital. "Time is not on your side," he had said. He explained that the longer I was in pain, the more that my body would get used to being in pain and the harder it would be to undo the brain's wiring of that habit. That advice must have seeped into my soul because I was on a mission to get to that workshop. I wasn't waiting until next month's workshop. I was going to the soonest workshop – the one that weekend.

My sense of urgency is echoed by a first century rabbi named Hillel who said, "Don't say when I have free time, I shall study, because you may never have free time."[23]

Like Hillel, I wouldn't wait until I had time to go to that workshop and learn more about my medical condition because time wasn't on my side. I had to reschedule a ceremony for Hannah and several of her scout troop members who had recently become Eagle Scouts. Thankfully, since they wanted me to be able to speak at and attend the event, the troop understood and allowed me to reschedule the event. They understood that my health had to come first. As the Talmud stated, "saving a life supersedes all (other obligations)."[24]

The workshop was attended by three men and three women (including me) who had come from all over the world to learn from Dr. Wise. One of the men was from Italy, and he had first travelled throughout Europe looking for treatments before eventually discovering this workshop and deciding to travel abroad to attend.

The workshop began with a day of learning by zoom, but then we gathered in person, and I started to get to know the other participants and hear their stories. Of the women who attended the workshop, I had been suffering for the shortest amount of time. I had been in pain for six months; the other two women had been suffering with pelvic pain for twenty years each. All three of us women were in our forties. Whereas my pain had started from surgery, the pain of the other two women had come out of nowhere – without a precipitating event – and was something they had been grappling with since they were in their twenties.

One of the women had considered attending the workshop several years earlier but had decided against it due to the cost. After a few more years of pain, she decided to come after all. When we talked, they were surprised that I had managed to find the workshop within just six months of having this problem. I felt like I had been suffering for so long, but they had been suffering for far longer.

During the workshop, the six of us spoke about some of the tough challenges that accompany this type of pain – particularly in relationships. One person was concerned about how their spouse would react to the idea that they couldn't have sex for the foreseeable future. Another had just started a romantic relationship and spoke openly about the challenge of talking to this new love interest about trying to find something they could do sexually even while he was in pain. One participant had never married or found a partner due to being in pelvic pain for their entire adult life. The pain was not only causing physical suffering but also clearly impacting the relationships of all concerned.

When I look back on the weekend, there are a few moments that stick out to me most vividly. The first was when I asked Dr. Wise how long this treatment plan typically takes. He responded that each person is different. The only way to know whether or when it works for you is to try it and see how long it takes to work. "But I would give it a year," he said.

'A year.' I thought to myself incredulously. I had already been in pain for six months. I couldn't imagine enduring a year more of this pain. How could I endure another year of not being able to sit down, of not being able to drive a car, or even be a passenger in a car, of being home-bound disabled, and dependent on others? I felt overwhelmed both by the time frame that he suggested as well as by

Ilana Grinblat

the number of hours per day that his treatment plan would take. I certainly couldn't do my job, take care of my kids and household responsibilities, and do the five hours of daily treatment he was suggesting – including stretches, trigger point releases, relaxation audio, reading, and videos.

Despite being very overwhelmed, I felt heartened at least to have a plan as well as to have talked with the other patients about their experiences and to have found support. Suffering with this kind of illness is lonely, especially when the doctors don't know what is wrong with you or how to fix it. Now, at least, I had a doctor telling me he knows what is wrong and how to fix it because he had fixed it for himself!

One evening, after the workshop concluded for the day, Tal and I went out to dinner in town at a charming restaurant which overlooked a river.

"I wish I had found this workshop sooner," I told Tal. "I could have saved myself months of pain." (By this point, I had been in the hospital three times over the six-month period. I had tried three nerve block procedures and seven bladder installations procedures that didn't work, had many tests and imaging, tried many doctors in two different hospital systems, all of which had been to no avail.)

"Can I turn it around on you?" Tal replied. "I'm glad you found the workshop now, instead of years from now."

This moment reminded me of an old Yiddish folktale which is found in a book called, *It Could Always be Worse* by Margot Zemach. Indeed, Tal's statement reminded me that as bad as my situation was, it could have been worse. I could have searched for many years before finding this workshop.

The folktale tells the story of a man who lived in a one-room hut with his wife, his six children, and his mother. The children were constantly bickering, and he felt cramped and frustrated. He turned to his rabbi for advice. The rabbi told him to bring his chickens into his home.

What Pain Teaches Us

With the chickens clucking in the house and feathers everywhere, life at home was even more messy, loud, and miserable. The man returned to the rabbi, who told him to bring his sheep and goats into the house as well. The home became even louder and messier. The man returned to the rabbi who told him to bring his cow into his house as well which he did. Finally, in complete exasperation, he returned to the rabbi who told him to remove all the animals from his home. Now, with only his wife, children, and mother, his home felt much more spacious and quieter, and they all slept soundly. The man returned to the rabbi and said:

> *Holy Rabbi, you have made life sweet for me. With just my family in the hut, it's so quiet, so roomy, so peaceful... What a pleasure!*[25]

Indeed, the past few years have been like a real-life version of this story where things got progressively worse and worse. Since, the pandemic began, losses accumulated, and the restrictions mounted. First, we had to cancel Hannah's bat mitzvah party. Then Cousin Stanley got Covid, spent seven weeks on a ventilator and died. Within a few days of Stanley's hospitalization, my aunt Laurie (in another part of the country) got Covid and was hospitalized and thankfully recovered.

As the pandemic progressed, the restrictions mounted – first they closed public places and we had to stay home, but we were allowed to walk outside in the neighborhood or to bike to the beach or the park. But then the beaches and parks closed too. Then when the fires came, and since the air was filled with smoke and ash, we couldn't go out of the house at all. And when the riots started after the killing of George Floyd, it was also too dangerous to go outside.

Then my health deteriorated. After my procedure, for five months, I couldn't sit down, and when I got Covid, I also couldn't walk and had trouble standing up. I even lost the ability to talk without having to pause to catch my breath. Certainly, the story of the last six months could easily have been entitled, *It Could Always Get Worse*.

Ilana Grinblat

Yet, this workshop offered a new beginning. Now after six months of searching, at least I had a diagnosis and a plan to get better. Perhaps it was like the moment when the rabbi told the man to remove the animals from his house. For me, the return to normalcy would not be as quick as the man who let all the animals out of his home and slept well that night. For me, it would come in stages – first the cows released, then much later the sheep, later the goats, and later the chickens let out of the house.

Step by step, constraints were lifted. In the hospital, I regained the ability to speak without having to stop to catch my breath. After leaving the hospital, I regained the ability to walk without the walker. Five months after the workshop, I regained the ability to drive. Six months after the workshop, I regained the ability to dance. With each day's stretches, my muscles slowly got more flexible and stronger. My pain slowly diminished over time.

As the restrictions gradually lifted, I faced the choice that the man in the story faced. I could become bitter and resentful about all I had been through, or I could choose to become grateful instead. What was normal for me before (being healthy and out of pain) could seem like an enormous blessing. Just being able to lie down on the floor beside my daughter and play a board game felt like a miracle.

I will always remember the speech that Gerda Weissman Klein, a holocaust survivor gave when she accepted the Oscar for her 1995 film *One Survivor Remembers* (which my father co-produced). She said:

> *Kary, Sheila, Sandy, Michael, my beloved husband, and my family. I have been in a place for six incredible years where winning meant a crust of bread and to live another day. Since the blessed day of my liberation, I have asked the question, why am I here? I am no better. In my mind's eye I see those years and days and those who never lived to see the magic of a boring evening at home. On their behalf I wish to thank you for honoring their memory, and you cannot do it in any better way than when you return to your homes tonight to realize that each of you who know the joy of freedom are winners. Thank you on their behalf with all my heart.*

In that moment, she reminded all viewers that even "a boring evening at home" is a blessing. Like the rabbi in the story who came to cherish being at home with his large and boisterous family, Gerda emerged from the horrors of the holocaust with abundant appreciation for her home and loved ones.

Likewise, Dr. Edith Eva Eger, who was in Auschwitz during the Holocaust, wrote in her memoir:

> *We can choose what the horror teaches us. To become bitter in our grief and fear. Hostile. Paralyzed. Or to hold on to the childlike part of us, the lively and curious part, the part that is innocent.*

At one point in the workshop, Dr. Wise said that one day when he was suffering with pelvic pain and couldn't sit down, he walked by a group of people eating at a restaurant who were sitting on hard chairs. He thought to himself, "They don't know how lucky they are."

Indeed! If/when I regain the ability to sit down again without pain, I hope I will remember how lucky I am.

Stubborn

August 12, 2022

"You're so stubborn." Tal told me.

We were in Philmont, New Mexico where I was serving as a chaplain for a couple weeks at a scout camp. Jeremy was also working there in the dining hall, and Hannah and Tal had joined us for a week to enjoy activities in the area. The main attraction in the area was a huge mountain called Tooth of Time. Jeremy, Hannah, and Tal were going to hike up the mountain with other scouts the next day, and I had decided to join them.

Tal didn't think I was well enough to go, and he had a point. I wasn't in much shape for scaling mountains. I was in a great deal of pelvic pain, and I was still on daily medicine to strengthen my breathing post-Covid. I wasn't the picture of health. Yet, the Tooth of Time was THE landmark that the place was known for – featured on all the t-shirts, posters, and postcards of the area. Climbing the Tooth of Time was the main attraction that everyone who went to Philmont talked about. I desperately wanted to go on the hike.

Like me, the Jewish people in the Torah were also accused of being stubborn. The phrase that is used is *am kasha oreph* – a "stiffed neck people."[26] This is generally considered an insult – indicating that they were inflexible and oblivious to what they could have seen if they would turn their neck to see the bigger picture. According to Chaim Potok, the term stiff necked is an image of obstinacy which comes from the farmer's experience with work animals. "When an animal's neck is stiff, it is hard for the driver using the reins to turn it in any direction."[27]

However, a rabbi named Ami considered being stiff-necked to be an asset. He wrote: "Is that a criticism? Rather it is to their credit."[28] That obstinacy is what has allowed the Jewish people to hold onto their faith even in perilous times. The people wouldn't turn their necks means that they wouldn't be swayed from what mattered to them. Stubbornness can be viewed as determination.

The hike was certainly a challenge, but I managed through the pain, and the views at the top were spectacular. I am glad that I ignored Tal's objections and went on the hike anyway, so I didn't miss out on that wonderful experience.

Tal was right. Somehow, this horrendous time has made me more stubborn, but I don't think that's a bad thing. Like the Israelites, I won't be deterred from my goals. Next time someone calls me stubborn, I'll consider it a compliment.

Just Breathe

September 8, 2022

 I went to see Doctor Shubov, who I hadn't seen in a few months, to see if he had any suggestions of further treatments to accelerate my healing. He gave me a few shots which didn't ease the pain. I updated him on my progress and showed him the stretches I do each morning. He said that he didn't have any further stretches to recommend. I was already doing them all. And he didn't have any new treatments to try.

 He gave me one piece of advice. He said that when I do my stretches, I should breathe deeply into them. He also said that I should do the stretches not because I have to (like a task on my to-do list) but because they feel good. He said that cats stretch because it feels good. He wanted me to stretch the way cats do. I explained that the stretches are painful, so it's hard to enjoy them. Still, he said that if I breathe into the stretches, it'll relax the muscles and make them stretch further.

 When I left the doctor's appointment, I felt disappointed. I had taken an hour-long bus ride in each direction for this appointment, and the shots which I was hoping would help didn't alleviate the pain. The only advice he had for me was to breathe. That idea seemed like not enough help to have spent a whole afternoon to have received.

 Despite my disappointment, I followed the doctor's directions. Early the next morning, I took a different approach to my stretches. Per the instructions from the pelvic pain workshop by Dr. David Wise, I usually do each stretch for thirty seconds. I checked and figured out that if I took the deepest breaths that I could, then five very deep breaths amounted to thirty seconds. So, as I did the stretches, instead of counting the seconds as I had been doing for the last five months, I took deep breaths and counted them instead.

I also put on the audio relaxation recording that I had received from Dr. Wise at the pelvic pain conference I had attended several months ago. The relaxation audio recording is supposed to be used while lying down, but I figured if it made a difference for the stretches for me to relax, then I might as well listen to the relaxation audio recording while stretching.

Doing my stretches that morning felt like a totally different experience than the way I had done the stretches every day for the five months prior. I was able to stretch more deeply and felt more relaxed which helped me with the pain of the stretches. Somehow, even though I had done the stretches every day for months, that morning, I felt like I was doing them for the first time. So, I must admit that Dr. Shubov was right again. The afternoon I spent wasn't wasted. He had given me transformative advice which opened up the experience in an entirely new way.

In Jewish tradition, there are two ideas which are central to prayer – and to life. These two ideas are opposites, but they are interdependent on one another. They say that opposites attract! Indeed, these two opposite ideas are deeply attracted, pulled, and connected to one another.

The two ideas are called *keva* and *kavanah*. *Keva* means fixed, and it refers to the idea that there are fixed times for prayer – (morning, afternoon, and evening) – and fixed liturgy (prayers assigned to each of those times). *Keva* encapsulates the idea that in Judaism, prayer is not just something that we're encouraged to do when the spirit moves us on rare occasion; rather it's a daily obligation that we're supposed to do three times a day. *Keva* is the idea that you shouldn't wait until you are inspired to pray because that inspiration may or may not ever come. Rather, you should pray whether you feel like it or not and even if you aren't in the mood, once you try it, you may get into it and find it meaningful.

The idea of *keva* applies also to study. As a first century rabbi named Hillel said, "Don't say when I have free time, I shall study, because you may never have free time."²⁹ *Keva* means making fixed times for study and for other important activities, built into your schedule, so you do them no matter what.

Still, according to Jewish tradition, *keva* alone is not enough. With *keva* alone, you can end up with a rote practice. If you're praying or studying because you have to, but your heart is not in it, then it's empty. That's where *kavanah* comes in. *Kavanah* means intention. It means the spontaneity of the heart. In addition to blocking out your schedule, you need to bring your spirit into the moment.

My favorite story which relates to *kavanah* has to do with the study of the Talmud. A student once told his teacher proudly that he had gone through the Talmud six times. The Talmud is 2711 pages long, and each page is dense and complicated. To even read through the Talmud once is an extraordinary accomplishment. If a person studies one double-sided page of Talmud a day which is hard to do, it takes seven years and five months to read through the whole Talmud once. To have read the Talmud six times was an extraordinary accomplishment!

When the student told his teacher that he had gone through the Talmud six times, the teacher replied, "Yes, but how many times has the Talmud gone through you?" The teacher understood that it wasn't enough just to read the words of the text. Only if the words go through you and permeate your heart and soul can they come to life and transform you.

This story encapsulates the relationship between *keva* and *kavanah*, *Keva* is going through the book; *kavanah* is when the book goes through you.

Essentially, the message that Dr. Shubov was conveying to me is that I had been stretching for five months as *keva* – as a fixed daily obligation – but that wasn't enough. I now need *kavanah*. If I put my heart, soul, and breath into the stretches, that would make all the difference.

In Judaism, the word *neshama* (soul) comes from the same root as the word *neshima* (which means breath). According to Genesis, God created the first person by blowing into the person's nostrils the breath of life and the human became a living being."[30] The mechanism by which the soul comes into the body is breath. That's why it's the same word. The importance of breathing which is true in Jewish tradition permeates Eastern religions as well and is central to the practice of meditation.

A spiritual teacher Eckart Tolle wrote that someone once showed him a brochure for courses of a spiritual organization and asked him which class he recommended attending. He replied that he didn't know because all seemed interesting. Yet, he added:

> *Be aware of your breathing as often as you are able, whenever you remember. Do that for one year, and it will be more powerfully transformative than attending all of these courses. And it's free.*[31]

As one of my healers always tells me, "Breathe with purpose."

There are two very different ways of living – one in which we count the seconds of our lives, and one in which we cherish every breath. By forcing us to stop working and be with the people we love, the Sabbath and holidays encourage us to switch over from focusing on our to-do list and frantically watching the clock, to cherish the miracle of our soul, our breath, and being alive.

In reflecting the centrality of breathing, I can't help but think of George Floyd's last words as he was being murdered. He said, "I can't breathe." And in essence, those three words sum up for me all the horror of the last three years.

Between all the racist, antisemitic, Islamophobic, homophobic, and sexist attacks and vitriol of the last few years, it's been very hard to breathe. We feel the pain and tension, never feeling safe and relaxed enough to breathe deeply. Covid literally makes it hard to breathe – and it made us watch our every breath to see who is breathing near us and whether they're going give us this disease. Wearing masks restricts our breathing to protect ourselves and each other. At the same time, air pollution and fires also make it hard for us here in California and for millions around the world to breathe.

After three and a half years of this kind of living, we are starved for breath. After years of living in isolation, we are starved for moments of simple joy – of just sitting with someone and sharing our life stories.

My blessing for us is simply: May we breathe. May we stop and smell the roses. After lots of *keva*, may we find some *kavanah*. As Dr. Shubov once told me, "Enjoy life. Doctor's orders."

The Dry Cleaner

September 16, 2022

As I prepared to lead High Holiday services for the first time in person after several years of leading them by zoom due to the pandemic, I searched through the back of my closet to find my High Holiday suits. On the Jewish High Holidays, it is customary to wear white (as a symbol of purity). So, I have several suits that are either white or beige for these occasions. When I found the suits in the back of the closet, I discovered that they were stained. I hadn't worn those suits in fifteen years – since the last time that I led High Holidays at Temple Beth Shalom which I was about to do again.

When I took the suits to the dry cleaner, the worker there said that he wouldn't take the suits because the stains weren't going to come out. I persisted and took them to another drycleaner who was willing to try to clean the suits but made it clear that they didn't guarantee that the stains would come out. If the stains didn't come out, I still needed to pay for the bill. I decided to take the chance.

When I came to pick up the suits a week later, the stains hadn't come out, but they were lessened. I could have worn them if I needed to, but as it turns out, they were too constricting. In my medical condition, I needed to wear clothes that have as little contact with my pelvic region as possible. I need flowy dresses that don't touch that area. I ended up paying for dry cleaning that didn't really work for suits that I can't wear now anyway. Oops!

This experience seemed to be a fitting metaphor at this moment, imparting important life lessons. Sometimes, if you leave stains in the closet for twenty years, they won't come out. And even if the stains do come out, you may find the outfit too constricting.

The same can happen in relationships or friendships. The longer that problems are left alone without being addressed, the harder they are to resolve. In time, the relationship can feel too restrictive and not fit anymore.

Similarly, as I returned to a job that I had held fifteen years ago, I was at first flooded with joy to be reunited with the families that I'd known and loved for over twenty years. When I stood to begin leading the High Holiday services on the pulpit which had been my home for five years (ending fifteen years ago), a wave of happiness came over me. "I'm happy," I said to myself and then to Tal. While I was happy to be back, as time moved forward, I also noticed the ways that I had changed in the last fifteen years. The traditional liturgy, which is very long, felt constricting to me. I was eager to explore alternative modalities of worship. Because of the pain, much as loved the congregants, I wasn't able to take on the job fully. I could lead particular services on dates when they needed coverage, but I couldn't take on the job of being their rabbi, not right now. The timing wasn't right. The suit didn't fit now.

I remembered a story in a book called *We Plan, God Laughs*, by a beloved and wise colleague and friend, Rabbi Sherre Hirsch. In the book, she explained that she was debating about a major decision in her life for over a year, "when enlightenment came via an unusual source, my favorite pair of jeans."

She explained:

> *My daughter was almost a year old before I was back to my goal weight and the whole time I couldn't wait to put on my favorite jeans. When it seemed the moment had finally arrived for their next pubic appearance, they just did not fit. I could not understand why. I had worn the jeans for years. I loved them. They were the good butt jeans, the skinny jeans. But now something was not quite right. As cute as they had once been, after three kids in four years, they just did not work any longer. I had to face it – I needed new jeans.*[32]

Rabbi Sherre too recognized this moment as a metaphor for other parts of her life. From the skinny jeans experience, she realized that the job she had loved before having children was no longer the right fit for her now that she was a mom. Even though she loved her congregants, it was time for a change.

Rabbi Sherre's words remind me of the story of God giving Moses the tablets containing the Ten Commandments on Mount Sinai. As Moses walked down the mountain with the heavy tablets, he dropped the tablets and they shattered. After begging God for forgiveness, God agreed to give Moses a second set of tablets.

God told Moses:

Carve out two tablets of stone like the first, and I will inscribe upon the tablets the words that were written on the first tablets, which you shattered.[33]

In the Torah, the words of the Ten Commandments on the second set of tablets were identical to the first.

Yet in life, I think that sometimes after a shattering experience, the words on our second set of tablets aren't the same as the words on our first set of tablets. When we break apart and get put back together again, sometimes the parts move around. The circuitry gets rewired. The parts are in different spots. The things we thought were true and right before don't fit the same way they used to, and we come to new truths, new lessons.

Physically, I found that my body as it healed wasn't getting back to exactly the way it used to be. Somehow, it was working differently. This was true emotionally and spiritually too. I am coming back different. Having spent the last ten months fighting to regain my life and health, I am coming back more assertive and realizing that my happiness is something I'm going to have to fight for as well. I feel less patient with settling for things as they are, and more eager to make whatever drastic, painful changes may be necessary in the short term to create a happier future down the road.

The healing process has changed my relationships. It drew me away from some friendships and relationships and towards others. My weakened state has left me with less strength to deal with people who are poisonous to my soul and made me thirsty for people who are kind and loving. Certain clear-cut truths that seemed so unshakeable to me before are shaky now. Other truths are emerging that are murkier but take into account the totality of my vulnerabilities and needs.

This process is profoundly unsettling. The physical changes cause emotional and spiritual crises. I am coming to see myself and others differently. The simple categories of good and bad, forbidden and permitted feel inadequate to the complexity of the experience at hand.

The Hebrew word for brokenness *mishbar* is from the same root as the word *mashber* which means birthing stool. I take comfort in the idea that the word for crisis and birthing stool are the related. I can only hope that from this brokenness, new possibilities are being born.

In a memoir called the *Book of Separation*, Tova Mirvis, recounts a theological crisis that she went through when she realized she no longer believed in Orthodox Judaism and went through a divorce with her husband. When she confided in a friend over coffee everything she was going through, the friend told her, "It's possible that the next half of your life may look very different from the first."[34] Indeed, her new life as a non-Orthodox woman differs greatly from how she lived her entire life until that point. Her second set of tablets hold different words than her first set of tablets. From the devastation, new truths emerged.

Rather than wearing my old suits, I wore my flowy flowered dress for the High Holiday services under my white *kittel* (robe)

. The dress wasn't white or beige. It was blue with pink flowers. It was a joyful dress, the one I had worn at my daughter Hannah's bat mitzvah two and a half years earlier, which took place on the last day that the last synagogue in Los Angeles was open before the entire city shut down for the Covid lock down. It was the dress I had worn on the last happy day that I had in the last two and a half years.

Wearing that dress, I was glad to be on the *bimah* (pulpit) and share the new truths that I had learned over these excruciating years. These sermons (which are included in this book) were by far the most personal sermons I had ever given – describing what I had learned from the pandemic, my medical disaster, and its aftermath. I shared the *mishbar* (birthing) that came from my *mishber* (crisis). From my heart, I shared words that were inscribed on my second set tablets, words that were very different from those on the first set of tablets that were shattered.

Broken Open

October 3, 2022

After ten months of pain, I was at my wits end. One of my healers was encouraged by the progress that I had made. Many of the muscles that previously were painful, such as my abdominal muscles, had released over time. However, the parts that remained painful – at the intersection of my buttocks and my thighs were critical because that's where sitting take place.

Whereas I could stand on a bus or a train, I still couldn't drive a car and even being a passenger in a car was painful. Living in Los Angeles, a city without good public transportation, I was limited to places I could walk and a few destinations that I could get to by bus or train. The logistics of my and my family's life were stressful. I was dependent on others to do even the simplest errands or tasks. After ten months of dealing with pain all day every day, with no end in sight, I was going out of my mind.

"In your medical opinion, is this going to be months, years, or forever?" I asked.

He said that there was no way to know. He added that I better find a way to get used to living like this, given that there is no way of knowing when this pain would end.

How could I get used to this? This was no way to live! It was SO hard, all day, every day.

Reflecting on this conversation, I remembered the moment twenty-seven years earlier when I realized that I wanted to become a rabbi. In my second year of college when I needed to decide my major, I had debated many different career options. I had many interests – writing, community building, counseling, teaching, Judaic ritual, dance. How could I pick between them?

Also, when I considered the biggest problems that the world was facing, I wondered: how best could I contribute? Certainly, the largest problem facing the world was environmental degradation, but science was not my strong suit. I thought that perhaps, I could be a psychologist. I remember having lots of conversations with my best friend Carla on the phone trying to choose a career path. I remember debating endlessly in my head, but I was stuck. I wasn't sure what to do.

At one point, I took a pen and paper and asked myself to write: What do you want to be when you grow up? And I wrote one word on the paper: "whole."

In my senior year of high school, my parents had divorced. My family had fallen apart in dramatic, catastrophic fashion, and during my first years of college, I was grieving. Feeling such brokenness, I longed for wholeness. I hoped to make a family of my own – to have children and give them what I hadn't had – a peaceful stable home (as well as the best of what I did have – such as travel and rich Jewish traditions). At that moment in college, I felt so broken and sad. I wanted the opposite of everything I felt and had experienced. I longed for wholeness.

When I wrote the word "whole" on that paper, somehow, I knew that meant that I wanted to become a rabbi. Being a rabbi meant that I didn't have to choose between my interests of writing, teaching, counseling, community building, and Jewish ritual. I could integrate them all into one – and thus attain wholeness.

Now, all these years later, in pain, I was facing the opposite prospect – that of making peace with the possibility of brokenness – for the foreseeable future, if not forever.

This conversation took place on the week of the Jewish High Holidays between *Rosh Hashanah* (the Jewish New Year) and *Yom*

What Pain Teaches Us

Kippur (the Day of Repentance). On these holidays, the cantor and the rabbi leading the service chant a prayer called *Hineni* (which means "Here I Am"). This prayer states:

> *Here I stand, impoverished in merit, trembling in the presence of the One who hears the prayers of Israel. Even though I am unfit and unworthy for the task, I come to represent your people Israel and plead on their behalf. Therefore, gracious, and merciful, awe-inspiring God, God of Abraham, Isaac, and Jacob, of Sarah, Rebecca, Rachel and Leah, I pray that I might successfully seek compassion for myself and those who sent me.*[35]

Although I had recited that prayer when leading High Holidays services for many years, reciting it on Yom Kippur that week, it resonated with me more deeply than ever. When I introduced the prayer, I explained that there are no saints in Judaism. In Jewish tradition, all people – even our religious leaders (and surely our biblical patriarchs and matriarchs) – are deeply flawed. The *Hineni* prayer recognizes that the cantor and rabbi who lead the service are "unworthy" of the enormity of the task of representing the community before God. To me, this meant that we are all broken people – trying to help other broken people find our way forward together.

Actually, that message is embedded in the holiday of *Yom Kippur* (the Day of Repentance). Exodus recounts that when Moses came down from Mount Sinai carrying the tablets of the Ten Commandments which God had given him, Moses saw the people worshipping the Golden Calf, the idol they had made while he was up on the mountain receiving the commandments from God. In dismay, Moses dropped the tablets, and they shattered. Moses then pleaded with God on the people's behalf for forgiveness and God gave Moses a second set of tablets with the Ten Commandments to bring to the people.

According to tradition, the day that Moses brought the second set of tablets to the people was the tenth of the Hebrew month of Tishrei (which is the date of Yom Kippur) each year. Thus, Yom Kippur is the holiday of second chances.

But what happened to the first set of tablets that were broken into pieces? According to the Talmud, the broken tablets were carried through the desert in the arc along with the new, second set of tablets.[36] This story contains a powerful message. Even the broken pieces were holy.

This idea contains great truth for our lives. As Rabbi Harold Kushner explained:

> *That which was once holy retains its holiness even when it is broken. So too the elderly, the senile, and the infirm may not be cast aside. They must be accorded the reverence they have earned in their lives.*[37]

Likewise, we don't discard the broken parts of ourselves, but we carry them around with us.

This idea also reminds me of a line in a novel by Mitch Albom. The passage is describing a moment in the life of a character named Annie when she is deeply depressed after her newborn baby died and her marriage was annulled. For the first few months, she was:

> *lying in bed during the daylight hours. She mourned her baby. She mourned her mother. She mourned her lack of imagination about the future. What purpose could make her leave this room? Every idea seemed small, inconsequential. She was broken open.*
>
> *But broken open is still open.*[38]

Indeed, after ten months of pain, I absolutely feel the experience has broken me. I can't see my way ahead. I often feel like I've lost my mind, my patience, my hope, and even my moral compass. When the pain gets strongest, I collapse in tears, feeling shattered.

At the same time, I do feel an openness that I didn't feel before. Writing my High Holiday sermons flowed more easily than ever before this year – because I was writing the Torah which was pouring out of my broken heart. Mitch Albom was right, "Broken open is still open."

I don't think I follow the instruction I was given. I don't think I can get used to living with this degree of pain and dependence on other people. But I can carry the broken pieces of myself around with me with the same reverence that the rabbis suggested the Israelites had for the broken pieces of the Ten Commandments. I can and do remind myself frequently that "broken open is still open," and I can cherish the openness and blessings that are coming in this excruciating time.

Indeed, whereas in college my goal of wholeness was understandable, the goal of broken openness may be more realistic. I can't give my children or anyone else perfection, or even wholeness. All I can give them is the love of my broken open heart.

Hot and Cold

October 7-10, 2022

My symptoms were flaring up for no apparent reason. I was suddenly in tremendous pain, so I got into the Jacuzzi, hoping this would help lessen the pain. At the weekend retreat with Dr. Wise, they often mentioned the value of heat and recommended taking a hot bath and using a heating pad to reduce symptoms, so I knew getting into the Jacuzzi and turning up the temperature was a good idea.

But it wasn't working. The pain was still going strong. As Friday night dinner approached, I couldn't get out of the Jacuzzi since the pain was so strong. Jeremy had come home from college for dinner, and I had cooked a special meal. The kids were hungry and restless, but I was out of commission.

Jeremy noticed that the water in the Jacuzzi looked green and suggested that Tal add chlorine to the Jacuzzi. Tal complied. Then suddenly, I felt like my legs and the entire lower half of my body were on fire. I jumped out of the Jacuzzi and ran to the shower, frantically trying to wash off the chlorine. My legs and abdomen were bright red.

"Are you okay?" Tal asked.

"No." I replied. "I'm definitely not okay. Look up what to do for a chlorine burn."

Hannah looked up the info and found that one should submerge in cold water and use aloe on the burn and take Advil for pain. I poured a cold bathtub, took Advil, told Tal and Hannah to go buy aloe and to leave Jeremy with me in case he needed to take me to urgent care or the hospital. I got in the cold tub and started to cry.

That night was the first and only night of my life that I ate *Shabbat* (Sabbath) dinner in the bathtub. Every time, I tried to get out of the cold bath, the pain became unbearable, and I got right back in.

I had cooked Cornish hen, potatoes, and artichoke with sauce. I had bought challah bread and grape juice. At my request, Jeremy, Tal and Hannah brought a small stool and put it next to the bathtub and fixed me a plate of food and glass of water. They set up a computer on the bathroom counter and created a zoom meeting, angled in such a way that my naked body was not visible, but I could see the kids and Tal, as they ate on the table in the backyard, as we usually do on Friday nights.

I was able to listen as Tal led the blessing for the children and the blessings over the wine and the bread that are traditionally recited each Friday night. I usually lead those blessings on guitar for the family, but not tonight. I just listened as Tal recited the blessing of the children (rather than putting my hands on their heads, blessing the kids, and kissing them as I usually do). It was easily the weirdest and saddest Sabbath dinner of my life.

Thankfully, though, I didn't have to go to urgent care or to the hospital. A few hours in the cold tub sufficed to cool down the lower half of my body enough. The redness lessened and then dissipated. The pain from the chlorine burn decreased enough for me to get out of the tub and go to sleep.

While in the tub, though, I noticed that I was able to sit without pain (whereas over the prior nine months, sitting always caused pain). For those couple hours in the freezing tub, the pelvic pain was gone.

I didn't know why the pelvic pain had disappeared in the tub. Perhaps, I thought that the pain from the chlorine burn was so strong that it eclipsed the pelvic pain and distracted my body so much that it couldn't process both types of pain at once. Ari (my doctor friend from college) had mentioned to me once that the body has trouble expressing different symptoms at once and that if one is stronger, another might be overpowered and might not be felt.

A few days later, I was talking with one of my healers who told me about Cryotherapy, a relatively new type of treatment where there's a freezing room that you go in for a few minutes to lessen the inflammation. I mentioned to him how the cold tub after the chlorine burn had helped with the pelvic pain. He suggested that I try Cryo.

That night, I was at target – getting Jeremy, Hannah, and me our flu shots, and on the shelf next to us as we waited for the pharmacist to prepare the shots, I saw the word Cryo. It was a Cryo ice pack suggested for pain. It cost $20. Since I had heard about Cryo and the pack had the word Cryo on it, I bought it.

When I got home, I stuck it in the freezer. For dinner, instead of standing for dinner because sitting was too painful, I sat on the ice pack instead – and it worked! Instead of being in pain, my butt was distracted by feeling freezing instead – which was a huge improvement. And it only cost $20! After spending thousands of dollars, having ten medical procedures that didn't work and countless medicines and treatments (most of which didn't work), the most game changing treatment only cost $20 and was one that I saw by happenstance. It was a miracle!

This moment reminded me of Hagar in the Book of Genesis and how when she was dying of thirst, God opened Hagar's eyes to see the well of water that was right in front of her. To me, seeing the Cryo pack at Target was like that miracle for Hagar. My eyes were opened to see something that had been there for months, but I hadn't seen it because I didn't know to look for it. Was it just a coincidence that I saw the pack on the same day that I learned about Cryotherapy? Honestly, I think it was a miracle.

The ice pack was a game changer for me. I discovered that with the ice pack, I could drive – which gave me my independence back after ten months of being dependent on other people to get me (and Hannah) where we needed to go. It was liberating and gave me hope for the future! I wouldn't be home-bound and disabled for the rest of my life (as I feared I might have been). What an enormous relief!

Ilana Grinblat

A few days later, I went to Cryo, as my healer suggested. It was quite the experience! At Cryo, they gave me a robe and asked me to go into a changing room, remove my clothing and put on a robe. They give me warm, long socks, earmuffs, and gloves and a mask (since we're still in the pandemic, after all). They also asked me to choose what song I would like to play while you're in the freezing chamber. I chose the 7 by Prince – which has a great beat and a great message about perseverance. Then I entered one very cold room, where I removed my robe and hung it up. (When I did this, I thought I must be crazy!)

Then I opened the door to the truly freezing room and a huge puff of freezing smoke comes at me. I stepped into the freezing room and closed the door. Then the music played, and I danced around so I wouldn't become a giant popsicle! The initial treatment is for two minutes, so the recording told me when each thirty seconds have passed, and then counted down the last ten seconds. After what felt like an eternity, the time was up, and I stepped into the adjacent room, put my robe back on as quickly as possible, and then stepped out to the main room – and got some hot tea.

Thankfully, this treatment helped too. On the ride to Cryo, I was sitting on the Cryo ice pack but still had significant pain. On the ride home from Cryo, that pain was much less. The freezing room was intense, but it was worth it. I felt the difference for several days, and I came back a week later when the pain got especially bad again, and again it helped. Together with the weekly muscle massage, my daily trigger point releases, exercises, stretching and swimming, I finally felt like I was getting somewhere. The uplift in my spirit was tangible and lasting.

When I reflect on this experience, I am struck by the fact that the chlorine burn (and the cold bath I took as a result) were what started this transformation. If I hadn't had the chlorine burn, I wouldn't have known how much cold could help me. Would I have tried Cryo with such urgency when my healer mentioned if I hadn't had the chlorine burn? Perhaps not.

So, the seed of the blessing of healing from Cryo was the pain of the Chlorine burn. If I had it to do over again, I wouldn't choose to have the Chlorine burn. It was awful! As with Rabbi Yochanan and Rabbi Hiyya Bar Abbah, my sufferings are not dear to me – not one bit! Still, I acknowledge that the hours of anguish from the chlorine burn led me to healing, in a way that I couldn't have known at the time that it happened until later.

As God had opened Hagar eyes in the wilderness after the angel asked caringly about her and reassured her, perhaps God opened my eyes at Target after my healer encouraged me to try Cryo.

In the Jewish prayer book, there is a blessing recited each morning which thanks God for "forming light and fashioning the darkness, making peace and, creating all." Actually, the earlier version of this prayer said, "forming light and fashioning darkness, making peace, and creating the bad." The last phrase was changed to make it more palatable. But the earlier version of the prayer raises powerful questions: Can we thank God even for the tough things in life? Can we find any blessings within the curses?

People often say things like: "Everything happens for a reason," or "God doesn't give people anything they can't handle." I instinctively revolt against all such simplistic, inadequate theological statements. Life often gives people suffering that no one could possibly be expected to handle. The Holocaust and slavery come to mind, just to name a couple examples.

One theological statement my father often repeated to us growing up is by Rabbi Irving Greenberg who said, "no statement, theological or otherwise should be made that would not be credible in the presence of burning children." I couldn't agree more.

Even apart from such historical atrocity, surely one couldn't say that the suicide of my friend's daughter "happened for a reason" or was something that anyone could be expected to "handle." Nor frankly was the agony of the last ten months something that happened to me for a reason or that I could be expected to handle.

Sometimes, people jump to quickly explain away other people's pain by saying that it's happening for a reason or will lead to blessings – rather than just acknowledging the depth of the anguish. The term

Ilana Grinblat

Pollyanna is used to mean that people tend to remember pleasant experiences more than unpleasant ones — to gloss over and minimize the pain. Personally, I am allergic to Pollyanna-ish theology.

Nonetheless in this case, I recognize that the blessing of finding the cold, healing treatments came from the pain of being burned.

Deuteronomy recalls how God told Moses:

> *See, this day, I set before you, blessing and curse, the blessing that you listen to the commandments of the One, your God, that I enjoin you this day, and the curse if you do not listen to the commandments of the One, your God, and turn away from the path that I command you today.*[39]

This passage makes it sound so simple — there are two separate paths — blessings and curses, and we just pick one. But it seems to me that it's not so clear-cut. Sometimes, blessings come in powerful disguises — and contain elements of curses in them. Other times, curses can contain the seed of blessings. This passage doesn't mention that sometimes the blessings are in the curses, and the curses are in the blessings. Life is messy. It's all mushed together.

Over the past year, the blessings and curses have come hand in hand. Even though this has easily been the worst and hardest year of my life, it has also contained extraordinary blessings — both professionally and personally.

At my job at the Board of Rabbis/the Jewish Federation, the support of my colleagues (the rabbis, interfaith and community leaders) was extraordinary during my illness — and my relationship to that job transformed positively during the year. Then, unfortunately, I resigned that position due to my failing health. Over the past month, I've started three new part-time jobs, all of which have been amazing blessings.

Personally, the healers that I've met to whom this book is dedicated have been incredible angels to me, and I've been opening up inside. Along with suffering, my writing and teaching is flowing as never before. If I could undo the pain of the past year, I would, but I can't. In fairness though, I should acknowledge that as intense as the curses have been, so too have been the blessings.

It is said that when a person loses one of their senses then their other senses are heightened. A person who loses their sight has an intensified sense of smell and touch. These heightened senses can be understood as a skill the person develops over time or as a gift from God or both. Perhaps, too, in times of sufferings, the blessings are heightened too.

As I write this chapter, it is the holiday of Sukkot, on which Jewish tradition tells us to read the book of Ecclesiastes by King Solomon, who lived in the mid-tenth century BCE and was known for his wisdom. Ecclesiastes contains a passage that like Deuteronomy sets out opposite qualities (like blessings and curses) in a simple and neatly divisible way.

Solomon wrote:

There is a time for everything,

and a season for every activity under the heavens:

a time to be born and a time to die,

a time to plant and a time to uproot,

a time to kill and a time to heal,

a time to tear down and a time to build,

a time to weep and a time to laugh,

a time to mourn and a time to dance,

a time to scatter stones and a time to gather them,

a time to embrace and a time to refrain from embracing,

a time to search and a time to give up,

a time to keep and a time to throw away,

Ilana Grinblat

> *a time to tear and a time to mend,*
> *a time to be silent and a time to speak,*
> *a time to love and a time to hate,*
> *a time for war and a time for peace.*[40]

Thirty centuries after writing this poem, Israel poet, Yehuda Amichai, (who lived from 1924-2000) disagreed with King Solomon. Amichai wrote an opposing poem, called, "A Man in His Life."

He wrote:

A man doesn't have time in his life
to have time for everything.
He doesn't have seasons enough to have
a season for every purpose. Ecclesiastes
Was wrong about that.
A man needs to love and to hate at the same moment
to laugh and cry with the same eyes,
with the same hands to throw stones and to gather them,
to make love in war and war in love.
And to hate and forgive and remember and forget,
to arrange and confuse, to eat and to digest
what history
takes years and years to do.

A man doesn't have time.
When he loses he seeks, when he finds

he forgets, when he forgets he loves, when he loves
he begins to forget.
And his soul is seasoned, his soul
is very professional.
Only his body remains forever
an amateur. It tries and it misses,
gets muddled, doesn't learn a thing,
drunk and blind in its pleasures
and its pains.

He will die as figs die in autumn,
Shriveled and full of himself and sweet,
the leaves growing dry on the ground,
the bare branches pointing to the place
where there's time for everything.

With all due respect to the wise King Solomon, I'm with Yehuda Amichai on this one. I too have found the blessings and the curses to be "muddled," mushed together, sometimes inseparably so. Pain and pleasure are separated by a hairsbreadth. In massage and in stretches, I discovered that often with just a breath, pain transforms into pleasure or vice versa. In a second, laughter turns to crying or crying into laughter. They're not polar opposites. They're close to one another.

Hot and cold, love and loss, forgetting and remembering, arranging and confusing are not as distinct as they seem. Losing one's way and finding one's way can come hand in hand. Over these last months, I've both lost my way and found my way, all at the same time.

Ilana Grinblat

Through all the messiness that is life, all we can do is thank God for the angels we find along the way – for the blessings that are *in* the curses and just maybe even for the curses that are *in* the blessings.

The Missing Piece

October 10, 2022

"May I have your permission to enter your energy field? Magdalena asked me on zoom.

From this question, I knew that I was in new territory.

"I have no idea what that means," I responded, "but yes."

Magdalena is a Reiki healer that my friend Deborah had recommended that I be in touch with to do a healing session for me. Deborah had explained to me what Reiki is in a few sentences. Reiki healers channel the energy of the universe into the places where there are blockages and pain to open up those spaces.

Honestly, this sounded totally wacky and not very credible to me. I was especially puzzled by the idea that it could be on zoom. My friend Carla had told me that Reiki involves laying hands on the painful parts of the body and using the heat of touch to bring healing energy that way. In that sense, I considered Reiki similar to massage with laser heat which I had been having every week for months and which was helping enormously. I thought: perhaps this was a gentler form of massage. But since one can't lay hands on a person by zoom, I doubted that any Reiki by zoom would work.

Still, after ten months of pain, I was desperate and at the end of my rope. I would try anything to get out of this pain. When Magdalena called me, I was crying because the pain had been especially bad for the last several days. So, when Magdalena suggested that we make a time to meet by zoom that night, I agreed.

That night, she met with me by zoom. After asking permission to enter my energy field, she proceeded to pray and then to be on zoom with me for an hour. I was lying on my bed with my eyes closed and she lied down on her bed. To be honest, I don't even know what she did or what happened, but I do know that it worked. The pain in my leg and my hips dissipated and was replaced by warmth. The next morning, (with the cryo ice pack) I was able to drive a car for the first time in ten months, and therefore regained my independence! I was jubilant!!

My journey of pain wasn't over by any means, but it was a turning point, which gave me much hope as well as self-sufficiency.

As a rabbi, I am supposed to believe in the power of prayer as well but honestly, this was my most direct experience of the healing power of prayer – or directing of the energy of the universe.

I called Deborah the next morning and thanked her for connecting me with Magdalena. I told Deborah that I hadn't believed that Reiki would work, that I still didn't know what had happened but was so grateful.

Deborah remarked that the energy of the universe is unseen and can be directed. "We believe in God, and that can't be seen," she reminded me. This was the same idea.

Indeed, I was reminded of something that Dr. Shubov had told me months earlier. He said that when the doctors didn't see anything wrong on the medical imaging (MRIs, etc.), they are tempted to think that nothing is wrong. But it was precisely what they couldn't see – the muscles – that was causing me such trouble.

So, if something unseen can cause such pain than perhaps, it's not such a stretch to believe that something unseen could bring healing too. Throughout these ten months, I had put more emphasis on the seen, on the physical dimensions of healing than on the spiritual ones. Each week, I had medical muscle massage. Each day, I did an hour of stretches, an hour of trigger point release with devices which Dr. Wise invented to push on the muscles, as well as an hour of swimming (with the frog kick that one of my healers recommended). I had tried

Cryotherapy which is a freezing room that you spend 2-3 minutes in to cool down the body. I had also tried acupuncture and different kinds of injections (as well as various medications). Other than acupuncture, all these techniques had helped enormously. I had focused on the physical dimensions of healing. But when it came to the spiritual part of healing, I had trouble motivating.

After the daily hours of the stretches, trigger point and stretches (which together including getting to and from the gym and having breakfast takes 4-5 hours), I had trouble motivating to spend the additional 2-4 hours daily that Dr. Wise recommends of audio relaxation exercises. I didn't want to quit all my professional and personal responsibilities to get this time into my day. I did some relaxation most days but nowhere near the recommended dosage. I preferred to spend an hour writing where I could see the effect of that hour by producing a chapter (which felt healing to me) than spend that hour listening to the relaxation audio which had no tangible result that I could see.

But perhaps by focusing (nearly exclusively) on the physical dimensions of my healing, I was missing something: the spiritual component – the unseen. (Perhaps as a rabbi, I should know better!)

From its first words to its last, the Torah teaches us that what is unseen can be more powerful than what is seen. God, which is unseen, can still have powerful effects in our lives. Certainly, though, it is frustrating not to be able to see God. Exodus chapter 33 recounts that Moses begged to see God. After so many years of working for God and so much struggle leading the Israelites through the desert, Moses wanted to be closer God, to see who he had been working for all this time. God refused, but offered Moses an indirect glimpse, saying:

> *I will make all My goodness pass before you, and I will call out before you the name of God, and I will be gracious and merciful to whom I will be gracious and merciful, but you cannot see my face, because no person can see my face and live. And God said, "See there is a place near me. Station yourself on the rock, and as my Presence passes by, I will put you in the cleft of the rock*

and shield you with My hand until I have passed by. Then I will take My hand away and you will see My back, but my face must not be seen.[41]

In explaining this passage, Rabbi Harold Kushner wrote:

> *What does it mean that a human being cannot see God's face but can see God's back? In the words of the Hatam Sofer, we cannot see God directly. We can only see the difference than God has made after the fact. We can recognize God's reality by seeing the difference God has made in people's lives.*[42]

Perhaps, what is true about God can also be said of healing. From my experience with Magdalena, I learned that healing is more complex and mysterious than I had realized.

Sometimes, we can't say what exactly is causing our healing, but we can only feel the effects and the difference it makes in our lives. All we can do is express gratitude for whatever healing has taken place and the sacred souls who have entered our energy field to make that possible.

The Power of Two

October 14, 2022

At services at Temple Har Shalom in Idyllwild, I shared as my sermon the prior chapter about breathing. Afterwards, a congregant, wellness instructor, dear friend named Kerry Abram shared with me several insights. First, she showed me how to breathe diaphragmatically, fully and deeply into my belly and ribs. She then explained that the latest scientific research for creating the most healing physiological state through breathing demonstrated the ideal rate as a mere six breaths per minute, with the exhale longer than the inhale.

Kerry also suggested that I could create this pace with each breath, and add to its healing power, by reciting the words of the prayer that Moses said when his sister Miriam was struck with a disease called *tzara'at*. The words of the prayer are: "*El na refa na la* (God, please heal her)."[43] This powerful prayer is six syllables, and therefore perfect to either do one breath per syllable or to slowly say all six syllables in one's mind during each breath.

Kerry shared how those words had brought her healing when she was in a ski accident years before. Kerry recounts her story as follows:

It's December 27, 2019, and I am…in…my…happy place. I am standing about 9,500 feet above sea level, preparing for my first ski run of a day the locals would describe as "a bluebird." The sky, like the avian adjective, is cloudlessly electric blue. Lake Tahoe spreads out before me as a massive

Ilana Grinblat

shimmering sapphire, perfectly earning its nickname as "The Jewel of the Sierra Nevada. My view expands almost 100 miles in every direction. I am filled with joy and belief in a Creative Intelligence behind it all.

I push off and ease into my first right turn when, suddenly, from the blind spot behind my right shoulder, comes an out-of-control snowboarder. He slams so hard into my boots that not only are both my skis knocked off, but I am catapulted up into the air, up the fall line (uphill), and then upside down, landing on my right shoulder and the right side of my face.

Sprawled across the ski run, screaming from the agony of blinding pain, a nearby ski instructor comes to my aid and calls the ski patrol. Sometime later they arrive to, slowly and gingerly, move me into a stretcher sled, and conduct the excruciating ride all the way down the mountain to await an ambulance. Once the additional pain of the transfer to the ambulance is complete and strong pain medication is administered, I mercifully pass out for the ride, the transfer into the Emergency Room and the subsequent examinations and tip-to-tail CAT scans to rule out brain and/or spinal injuries.

I awaken to Emergency Room Physician Raymond Stillwell bursting into my examination room. "Kerry, you have a badly broken shoulder, but I don't care about that now. Cover your left eye and tell me how many fingers I am holding up." I respond, "My eye must be swollen shut. If you pry it open, then I can tell you." The Doctor firmly replies, "No Kerry. Your facial fractures have created a massive hematoma (blot clot) inside your skull, and it is pressing on your optic nerve creating temporary blindness in that eye. The pressure has already gone on long enough to possibly kill the nerve in that eye and permanently blind you. I need to immediately cut tendons in your eye to try to relieve that pressure and then put you in a helicopter to the Trauma Center in Reno."

Almost instantly a huge hypodermic needle administers some bit of anesthetic; then the knife; then the blood flies and flows everywhere; then the gurney begins to roll fast down a hallway as a nurse runs alongside applying bandages; then doors burst open into the sharp cold afternoon air of the helicopter pad. The Flight Nurse loads me in and says, "I will be right here with you for the whole 22-minute trip". My left eye is crying with pain and fear.

Two thoughts rapidly alternate: "I'm blind." "22 minutes." "I'm blind." "22 minutes." I feel my hysteria growing inside despite the supposedly calming narcotics. What to do? I am firmly strapped helplessly onto the stretcher. No action possible. How to cope? How to cope? And just then, the ingrained daily habits of the last decade kick right in and I know exactly what I must do. PRAY! Pray like my life and sanity depends upon it, because at this moment, they literally do.

Ah-na-el-na-ray-fa-na-la. The most powerful healing prayer in the Torah — the Hebrew prayer Moses used to instantly and miraculously heal his beloved sister Miriam when she fell ill during their 40-year desert wanderings. Over and over and over, with the concentration only deep desperation can prompt. The flight seemed to take both 22 years and just moments.

We land. My stretcher is rapidly transferred to a wheeled gurney, rushed through the doors of the hospital helipad and into a massive trauma treatment room like I had only ever seen on television. An ophthalmologist approaches my head, covers my left eye, and removes my thick, blood drenched bandages. After an endless moment of inspection, she slowly says, "Kerry, tell me how many fingers I am holding up."

I begin to sob. I can barely speak. Finally…I manage to blurt out possibly the most meaningful word I have ever spoken — "Two!"

I was so moved by Kerry's story and her advice that the next morning when I did my stretches, I breathed and repeated the words in my mind with each stretch, *"El na refa na la."* Each subsequent morning when I did my swimming at the pool interspersed with the stretches, with each breaststroke I would say in my head one of the syllables of *"El" "na" "re" "fa" "na" "la,"* and with each stretch, I repeated *"El na refa na la"* in my head. Certainly, my mind would wander to what I needed to do that day, but when I noticed that my thoughts had strayed, I would try to return to the refrain of *"El na refa na la,"* again and again.

In the Talmud, the rabbis listed the obligations of a father in raising a son. They taught:

Ilana Grinblat

> *A father is obligated regarding his son to circumcise him, and to redeem him, and to teach him Torah, and to marry him to a woman, and to teach him a trade. And some say: also, to teach his son to swim.*

Why is teaching swimming on the list of the six core responsibilities from a father to a son? Some of the explanations I've heard are because learning to swim can be a matter of life and death and/or because learning to swim cultivates independence. Both these reasons are certainly true. Surely, making sure my children learned to swim was a critical task upon me as a parent. I thought of this teaching often when taking my kids to swim lessons.

Yet, my experience swimming while repeating the "*El na re fa na la*" prayer in my mind every morning before dawn brought new meaning to the teaching in the Talmud for me. This practice transformed the whole hour and fifteen minutes of swimming and stretches into a prayer and a meditation. With each movement, I tried to imagine that God was healing me – that God and I and my team of healers were working together to bring me back to health and to life.

The pool became like a *mikvah* to me – the ritual bath that Jews use to mark important life cycle moments such as a wedding or a conversion. The swimming helped me to regain the strength of my breathing and energy level post-Covid and stretched my muscles to reduce my pain. Over the months of swimming, I grew stronger both in body and spirit. Perhaps the father was obligated to teach his son to swim not only to save his life but also because swimming can be a form of prayer and a powerful mechanism for healing.

Another dear congregant of mine, Yetta Kane from Temple Beth Shalom is celebrating her ninetieth birthday this weekend. She is a Holocaust survivor, an indomitable spirit, and an inspiration to all who know her. I had the joy and honor of co-officiating for five years with her beloved husband Rabbi/*Hazzan* (Cantor)/Dr. David Kane, of blessed memory. Yetta once shared with me that someone asked her about driving after her husband had died. "You still drive alone at your age?" the friend asked incredulously. "No," Yetta replied. "I never drive alone. Whenever I drive, *Hashem* (God) and my sweetheart are in the car with me. Whenever I start the car, I say to them, God, sweetheart, let's go for a ride. I am never alone."

Yetta told me this story years ago and it always stuck with me. As Yetta doesn't drive alone, I don't swim alone either. I swim with my healers and doctors who taught me this regimen of stretches and encouraged me to swim daily. I swim with God, the ultimate catalyst of healing and transformation.

When Kerry opened her eyes after her accident, she said the word "two" – which may have been the most meaningful word she said in her life. Indeed! Again and again, throughout my healing process, I've discovered the power of two – the way that a story or suggestion from a congregant, friend or healer will take me to the next crucial step toward healing. As Yetta's story reminds me, although illness can make us feel lonely, we are not alone in our healing.

As the Indigo Girls sang:

Adding up a total of a love that's true,
Multiply life by the power of two.

Yes and No

October 19, 2022

"Breathe," one of my healers said, as he gently pushed my leg up high in the air, stretching it beyond where I felt it could go, and I felt the pain burn at my thigh. My leg was resisting being pushed so far.

"You have to trust me," he said gently. I tried to breathe into the stretch.

"I do trust you," I said, "but it hurts."

"I know it hurts," he said quietly.

The next day I led a joyful baby naming for family members in Long Beach. The following day, I taught Torah study in the morning and led a potluck dinner, Torah study session, and led a sing-along on guitar and was feeling great. Maybe, I had turned a corner. Just maybe, I was approaching the end of the tunnel of the pain.

The next morning, I started leading Shabbat services feeling fine, but as the pages went by, the pain got worse and worse. I asked a knowledgeable lay leader named Sam to come to the *bimah* (podium) and take over for a few minutes so that I could go take a painkiller. Even once I took the pill and did some stretches in my office, I couldn't get the pain to go away. When the pain flares up, there's a sound that I make that sounds like sneezing. I couldn't get the sneezing sound to stop, and I couldn't lead the service while making that noise every few seconds. I laid down in my office and waiting, hoping for the pain to stop in time for me to give my sermon.

I was shocked by the pain which seem to come out of nowhere, after I'd had such a good day the day before. But I probably shouldn't have been surprised.

It had been a busy week, a busy month for that matter. It was the last week of the Jewish High Holiday season, and I had been officiating in three different congregations. The prior weekend, I had lead services at Temple Har Shalom of Idyllwild, where I serve as the rabbi by leading services one Sabbath per month. Then on Monday morning, I led services at Temple Beth Shalom of Long Beach. Monday night, I danced at Simchat Torah with Open Temple, where I was beginning a job as education director. On Thursday, I was back in Long Beach to officiate at a baby naming and Friday morning and evening, I had led teachings at Open Temple. So, Saturday morning, when I led services in Long Beach, I guess my body was saying it had enough. I was down for the count.

Each of the places where I am working are beloved to me. Temple Har Shalom of Idyllwild is a gorgeous place with huge trees and a quaint, relaxing atmosphere and delightful people. I had applied there years prior to lead High Holiday services because I had heard from a colleague that he loved going hiking in Idyllwild. I figured that if the town was pretty with good hiking, then that would be a great place to spend the holidays, and it was! It was beautiful there and I fell in love with the congregation right away. When they asked me to lead services not only on the High Holidays but also once Sabbath a month, I loved the idea of getting away to this idyllic place regularly. I gladly agreed.

I also loved Open Temple in Venice, CA. While Idyllwild is nestled beautiful tree covered mountains, Open Temple is near the beach and the Venice Canals – which I also love. I had met Rabbi Lori Shapiro, the founder of Open Temple in our first year of rabbinical school (when she was Lori Schneide). We had created a dance troupe together and performed an interpretive piece about our year of rabbinical school for our classmates and teachers. We were kindred, creative spirits – bonded by our love of dance, the arts, and Torah. After the first year of rabbinical school, Lori transferred to a different rabbinical school on the East Coast. Once she graduated, she returned to California and founded Open Temple, I was thrilled to attend the services and events there over the years and get involved in the community. When she told me about the opportunity to become the education director, the position was such a perfect fit that my cover letter was so easy to write that practically wrote itself. I was so excited!

Temple Beth Shalom of Long Beach was the congregation I had served for five years beginning one year after I became a rabbi. I was there for a few years as a newlywed and then both my son and my daughter were born during the time that I was the rabbi there. The bris and baby naming ceremonies welcoming Jeremy and Hannah into the world and into the Jewish community both took place in that sanctuary. I love the people of the congregation. We had celebrated the highs of life and mourned the low moments together for decades.

Shortly after my daughter was born, I left the congregation so that I could be around more to raise our children. In my farewell dinner, I told the congregants that even though I wouldn't be working there anymore, I would always be their rabbi. In the subsequent fifteen years, I still officiated at funerals, and key lifecycle moments of congregant's lives. In my heart, I never really left. So, fifteen years after I left, when they asked me to return as their rabbi, I was delighted. My son was off at college, my daughter was busy with her afterschool tennis team. I was available and jumped at the chance.

The problem was that all these opportunities that I had dreamed of for years came through precisely as I was falling apart physically. By some miracle, I was able to do the scheduling such that the three part-time jobs didn't overlap. I could take them all. Plus, I was getting stronger. I hoped that sometime soon I would be out of pain and back in business.

Each of these jobs were brand new. I didn't know how they would turn out. Although I loved my friend Lori, I wasn't sure how it would be to work for her. I also didn't know how it would be to be back at Temple Beth Shalom after fifteen years away. The Idyllwild congregation had only as small group of members, and it wasn't clear whether it would continue. So, I figured that I shouldn't put all my eggs in one basket. I should hedge my bets in case one or more of these opportunities fell through. I hated making big decisions, disappointing people that I love, and turning down great opportunities. I thought that if possible, accepting all these amazing positions would be ideal.

After that morning on the *bimah* (pulpit), I realized that out of love, and out of hope and optimism that my health would improve, I had made a mistake. I had overcommitted myself professionally. I couldn't serve as the rabbi of three different, geographically dispersed, congregations while being this sick. My daily trigger point releases, stretches, and swimming take four hours every day (which I usually start at 3:00 AM) since I have trouble sleeping, which means that I am constantly very tired. In addition, I have weekly medical massages and other medical appointments. When I have time, I write this book which helps to process the struggles that I am going through. The writing feels healing to me.

I remembered a quote from a podcast that I had listened to a while back on the Ten Percent Happier app. The person being interviewed was a writer who talked about how she is often approached with wonderful professional opportunities which she chooses to turn down to focus on her main professional passion which is her writing. She said, "Your no makes room for your yes."

Indeed, in Jewish tradition, there are 613 commandments. These are comprised of 248 positive commandments (actions we are supposed to take light lighting Shabbat candles or giving charity) and 365 negative commandments (actions we are supposed not to do – such as murder or stealing). The positive and negative commandments are deeply intertwined and interdependent. For example, on the Sabbath, the actions we abstain from such as working, give us the time for the actions we take on Shabbat such as meals with family and friends, and services. By turning off the computer, we are more present with our loved one on the Sabbath.

The Ten Commandments appear twice in the Torah – once in Exodus and once in Deuteronomy. Each time that the fourth commandment -- the injunction to keep the Sabbath -- is mentioned a different verb is used. In Exodus, God said, "Remember the Sabbath Day and keep it holy."[44] In Deuteronomy, God said, "Guard the

Sabbath and keep it holy."[45] Most of the wording of the Ten Commandments is identical in both places. So, why these two different formulations of the fourth commandment?

The rabbis understood the word *Zachor* (remember) in the Exodus version to refer to the positive commandments that we're supposed to do on Shabbat and the word *Shamor* (guard) in the Deuteronomy version to refer to the negative commandments that we're supposed keep ourselves from doing on the Sabbath. A prayer sung on Friday night called the *L'cha Dodi* (Come, my beloved) states that these two words *Zachor* (remember) and *Shamor* (guard) were said by God at once – as one utterance. Indeed, this idea echoes the one that the writer said in the podcast. Our yeses and our no's go together. Our no makes room for our yes.

The night after leading services in Long Beach, I reached out to the lay leaders of the congregation and told them that given how much pain I was in, I didn't think that it was wise for me to lead services the following Saturday, as I had planned. I asked whether anyone else could lead the service that day.

I knew in my heart that night that I wouldn't be able to accept the job at Temple Beth Shalom. (On the edge of tears, I wrote this chapter that night.)

As much as I loved the congregants in Long Beach and hated to disappoint them, I would have to say no to say yes to my healing. Two days later, I spoke with the leadership of Temple Beth Shalom, and we agreed that I wouldn't accept the position at this time; they would need to look for another rabbi.

I couldn't hedge my bets. I have to put all my eggs in Open Temple's basket. I could keep one egg in Temple Har Shalom's basket, to enjoy a quiet, healing getaway each month, but the rest of my eggs would have to be in the basket of Open Temple which was closest to my home.

When I was in Idyllwild that weekend, my congregant and friend Kerry and I sat outside on her home's deck, overlooking the trees, mountains, and clouds, and talked about different kinds of faith. She shared the notion that the Hebrew word *Emunah* means faith in an abstract way – believing that God created and continually creates the world, while the Hebrew word *Bitachon* means trust in a personal way – trusting that God will take care and guide me in my daily life.[46]

This quality of *bitachon* (trust) is one of Maimonides' categories of friendship, chaver *bitachon* (a friend of trust). This type of friendship is the second to highest level in Maimonides' hierarchy, one above a *chaver hanachat* (a friend of satisfaction). He explained:

> *A friend of trust is a friend that you can trust your soul with, without keeping anything from that person in action or in speech, and one reveals to that friend all his matters, both good and bad, without worrying about being embarrassed by that friend either in private or in public. When a person can trust that friend so thoroughly, one will find great joy from talking to that friend and in that friendship.*[47]

In reflecting on my conversation with Kerry, I realized that I had *emunah* in Lori – faith in an abstract way; otherwise, I wouldn't have taken the job at Open Temple. But now, I would need to have *bitachon* in her – to have the deeper trust to really put my eggs in her basket, to pour my soul into her care and into Open Temple. Lori had been my *chaverah hanachat* – a friend who brought me joy – for years. Now, I would need to decide that she would become a *chaverah bitachon* – a friend who I trust.

As I chose to trust my healers, I would have to choose to not only to love Lori but also to trust her, even when it hurts – even when she regularly pushes me outside of my comfort zone. Only by trusting my healers can I let them to stretch my legs beyond where they want to go. So too, only by really trusting Lori could I stretch and grow to new heights as a rabbi and a teacher.

I also need to develop a deeper *bitachon* in myself and listen to my body when it tells me that it needs to rest. For now, I need to be less optimistic about when healing will come and more realistic about my limitations.

I also need to listen better to my soul when it tells me what direction to go in life – even if that direction is very different from what I had planned. Only by saying no to my past, can I say yes to what I hope will be a better future ahead.

What Remains

October 20, 2022

After ten months of constant pain with no end in sight, to say that I have run out of patience is an understatement. I lost my mind a long time ago. But for the first time in this ordeal, I have some words to hang onto. I feel like someone treading water in the middle of an ocean of pain, but these words offer a rope to a lifeboat.

One of my healers told me that he thinks I'm dealing with about ten to twenty percent of the pain level that I was dealing with when I first met with him five months ago. This statement comforted me. I like having a number to keep in mind. It's hard for me to gauge my pain level. The pain doesn't give me a Richter scale to measure my progress. For me, being in pain seems like being pregnant. You either are or you're not. When in pain, all I want is to be OUT, now if not sooner.

Still, it's hard for me to focus on the progress that I've made because the pain that remains is so debilitating. The pain that remains is in my buttocks and the top of my legs, so it is still painful to sit down – which is so critical to driving or riding a car. I miss being able to sit with Hannah and play a board game or sit for lunch with a friend at a restaurant. My workdays feel longer since I'm on my feet the whole time and so I don't have the stamina that I used to have. I'm tired of being tired.

My *chevruta* (friend and study partner), Rabbi Rachel Bovitz sent me a book as a gift in the mail. The book is entitled *The Choice* by Dr. Edith Eva Eger, about her experiences during the Holocaust and throughout her life. In this memoir, Dr. Eger described the horrors of her time in Auschwitz. Shortly after arriving at the concentration camp, Edith's mother and father were both murdered. Edith and her sister's heads were shaven, and they were stripped of their clothes. At that moment, standing naked and bald, her sister Magda, spoke to her and said:

"How do I look?" she asks. "Tell me the truth."

At that moment, Edith faced the dilemma of how to respond to her sister. She recounted:

> *The truth? She looks like a mangy dog. A naked stranger. I can't tell her this of course, but any lie would hurt too much and so I must find an impossible answer, a truth that doesn't wound. I gaze into the fierce blue of her eyes and thank that even for her to ask the question, "How do I look?" is the bravest thing I've ever heard. There aren't mirrors here. She is asking me to help her find and face herself. And so I tell her the one true thing that's mine to say."*
>
> *"Your eyes," I tell my sister, they're so beautiful. I never noticed them when they were covered up by all that hair." It's the first time I see that we have a choice to pay attention to what we lost or to pay attention to what we still have.*
>
> *"Thank you," she whispers.*[48]

I was struck by Eva's incredible ability in that moment to shift her and her sister's focus from all they had lost to what they still had.

This story reminded me of a true story about master violinist Itzhak Perlman. Perlman was struck with Polio as a child and has used leg braces and crutches to assist in walking ever since. Rather than being seated before the entrance of the orchestra, Perlman walks independently onto the stage during the performance.

> *With the help of his crutches and braces, Itzhak Perlman slowly walks the breadth of the stage, takes his seat as first violinist, bends down to undo each*

brace, places his crutches on the floor, picks up his violin and then with a nod to the conductor, he begins the evening's musical performance.[49]

In New York City in 1995, one of his violin strings broke halfway through the concert. Based on this performance, Rabbi Harold Schulweis of blessed memory wrote a poem entitled Playing with Three Strings. This poem is found in *Dancing on the Edge of the World*, a wonderful book edited by my teacher and colleague Dr. Rabbi Miriyam Glazer.

> *We have seen Yitzhak Perlman*
> *Who walks the stage with braces on both legs,*
> *On two crutches.*
>
> *He takes his seat, unhinges the clasps of his legs,*
> *Tucking one leg back, extending the other,*
> *Laying down his crutches, placing the violin under his chin.*
>
> *On one occasion one of his violin strings broke.*
> *The audience grew silent but the violinist did not leave the stage.*
> *He signaled the maestro, and the orchestra began its part.*
> *The violinist played with power and intensity on only three strings.*
>
> *With three strings, he modulated, changed, and*
> *Recomposed the piece in his head*
> *He returned the strings to get different sounds,*
> *Turned them upward and downward.*

Ilana Grinblat

The audience screamed delight,
Applauded their appreciation.
Asked later how he had accomplished this feat,
   The violinist answered.
   It is my task to make music with what remains.

A legacy mightier than a concert.
Make music with what remains.
Complete the song left for us to sing,
Transcend the loss,
Play it out with heart, soul, and might
With all the remaining strength within us.

The examples of Dr. Eger and Itzhak Perlman remind me that instead of focusing on the amount of pain that I have left, that I should focus instead on how far I have come. They inspire me to shift from comparing my current state of pain to my prior, pain-free body, but instead do the best I can with my remaining strength. Sometimes to comfort myself, I even recite a list in my mind of all my body parts that are working properly (my heart, my lungs, etc.). This practice transfers my attention from the bodily capacities I have lost (such as the ability to sit) to those I still have.

One of my healers said that he thinks that if I keep doing what I'm doing that I may be out of pain in January (which is two and a half months from now). I hang onto his words. It is the first time in the last ten months that any medical professional has said the phrase, "out of pain," and offered any possible time frame for that possibility. These words offer the possibility of a light at the end of the tunnel.

Every weekday morning at 5:00 AM and every weekend at 8:00 AM when the gym opens, I am there, swimming and doing all the stretches that were given to me by my team of healers and doctors. I swim one lap between each stretch, so the combination of stretches and swimming takes an hour and fifteen minutes each morning. I am working hard to meet – and dare I dream even beat – my healer's time estimate for my recovery.

Each day, I hope I am getting one step closer to leaving the prison of pain. Someday, I hope to dance again. In the meantime, I'll make music with what remains.

The Shift

November 22, 2022

In honor of the one-year anniversary of Esther's death, my friend Deborah convened a Sound Healing and Yoga Nidra class led by healer and teacher Alison Ungaro. I had never been to such a class before and wasn't sure what to expect.

The class began with a meditation where we were encouraged to picture rainbow colored light flowing through different parts of the body. At another moment, Alison asked us to picture ourselves by a lake looking out at a field full of wildflowers. I enjoyed the vivid visual images that she gave us and found it more engaging than other types of meditation that I had tried.

Then the sound healing part of the class began. Alison used spoons and bowls to make ringing reverberate throughout the room while we closed our eyes. I found the sound mesmerizing and a little unsettling too. At one point, I started to worry whether the ringing in my ears would continue, even when the sound bath was over. Would I regain regular hearing again? Could this loud ringing damage one's ears? As it turned out, my worry was for naught. As soon as the sound healing was over, my hearing immediately went back to normal.

At one point in the sound healing, I felt a small shift in my left leg and hip. Throughout the last many months, both of my legs and hips hurt, but my left leg was considerably worse than my right. The shift in my left leg was small but very tangible. It felt like my leg had suddenly moved back into place.

Ilana Grinblat

I wasn't magically healed after that. I still had pain, but that moment marked a very clear turning point. I walked more normally after that, and the pain started to decrease. With the help of my continued daily stretches and swimming, weekly massage, and an infrared light pad recommended by Dr. Brian Ellinoy, the pain decreased dramatically.

That momentary shift felt like a miracle — which propelled me toward healing, toward the light at the end of this year-long, dark, excruciating tunnel. As with Reiki with Magdalena, this moment didn't involve physical exercise or touch, but somehow the sound bath washing over me propelled my leg to move. This class was a spiritual experience which led to physical healing.

Before shooting an arrow, adjusting your aim on your bow even slightly causes the arrow tol land in an entirely different place. The rabbis use this metaphor as a way of thinking about the High Holidays. Making small adjustments in our personal aim during the High Holidays can change the trajectory of our year — and therefore of our life. Likewise, that small shift in my leg during the sound healing changed the arc of my life from pain to healing.

At the end of class, we took Iris flowers and created a mandala — a circle of flowers — in memory of Esther Iris Blum. Then, we stood in a circle around the flowers, and each took a pink slip of paper from a jar and read the quote on our paper to one another. The quote that I received was by Dutch Catholic priest and theologian Henri J. M. Nouwen. It read, "Joy does not simply happen to us. We have to choose joy and keep choosing it every day."

This quote encapsulated the spiritual lessons of this year which has been marked by abundant pain, loss, and heartache. It was a year of walking up each morning before dawn and driving to the gym to fight for life and towards healing. It was a year of walking with friends and talking through the struggles. It was a year of cherishing the blessings of the people who unlocked the doors of the prison of pain — who solved one piece of the puzzle, and who supported and cared for me during my illness. Together, we worked to free each other from our respective prisons of pain. Now, the challenge remains to keep choosing love, blessing, and joy every day.

A Time to Dance

December 20, 2022

It was December 20th, 2022. The one-year anniversary of the procedure. What a depressing milestone. The polyp removal was supposed to be a minor procedure that may cause a little soreness the next day, but here I was a year later still in constant pain.

Surely, I was much improved. I had regained the ability to drive. I was no longer homebound and as debilitated as I had been. I could see the light at the end of the tunnel even if I wasn't there yet. But still, it was upsetting to know that a year had passed, and the pain was still with me with each day.

It was the third night of the holiday of Hanukkah. Open Temple had been asked to lead the Hanukkah candle-lighting at the Third Street Promenade in Santa Monica. The week before I had taught the Creative Torah Academy students a Hanukkah dance. It was my first time teaching a dance since the procedure. Even though I was in pain, I was able to dance, and I was grateful. When Rabbi Lori heard that I had taught a dance to the students, she asked me to prepare a few Hanukkah dances to lead at the celebration.

At the promenade, we set up a table with dreidels and handouts about Open Temple and greeted those who walked by. Rabbi Lori led the candle lighting blessings, and we lit the big menorah. Open Temple's musician-in-residence, Idan, led Hanukkah songs on guitar. After an hour, I thought that Rabbi Lori had forgotten about the idea of my leading dancing. I didn't want to remind her, feeling shy about

Ilana Grinblat

it and concerned whether the pain would make it hard to dance. But then she asked me to lead the dancing.

We put the music on. The song was called "Miracle" by The Maccabeats. I started the dancing. Rabbi Lori and a few others joined in. A young girl came up to the podium and danced behind me, following along with the choreography.

The dancing lifted my spirits. Although I wasn't out of pain, I had come a long way. Six months earlier, I had been in the hospital, barely able to walk with a walker, running out of breath in the few steps to the bathroom, and here I was leading dancing for kids and adults. It was a miracle indeed. Surely, there was no better way to mark this one-year milestone.

I recall the words of King Solomon:

> *There is a time for everything,*
>
> *and a season for every activity under the heavens:*
>
> *a time to be born and a time to die,*
>
> *a time to plant and a time to uproot,*
>
> *a time to kill and a time to heal,*
>
> *a time to tear down and a time to build,*
>
> *a time to weep and a time to laugh,*
>
> *a time to mourn and a time to dance,*

There have been many tears over the past year. Now, the time has come to dance.

Year Two

The Setback

December 23, 2022

(date of procedure)

In the days after the Hanukkah celebration, I thought I was in the home stretch of the pain. I was improving greatly. I could see the light at the end of the tunnel and was moving towards it swiftly. Several months before, one of my healers had said that if I kept doing what I was doing, I could be out of pain in January. Now, January was only a week away. I felt hopeful and buoyant.

Then I suffered a setback in the pain. I had a colonoscopy. The doctor had strongly recommended that I have one at my age. Due to the pain of the past year, I had put it off for fear of intensifying the pain. But I felt stronger now. My healers felt that I was strong enough now and that I would be okay.

Although I was scared of the procedure, I also didn't want to take a chance of having polyps that needed to be removed or colon cancer. We had lost a beloved cousin to colon cancer several months prior. Also, unlike the polyp removal on my cervix, I knew that I didn't need to be awake for this procedure, so hopefully my muscles wouldn't tense up as a result.

Despite my fears, I did all the preparation for the procedure and went through it. I was hoping that the colonoscopy would mark the beginning of the end of the medical nightmare of the past year. I would get through this procedure, and then I'd be in the home stretch of healing and get the rest of the way out of the prison of pain.

Ilana Grinblat

When I first woke up from the procedure, I didn't feel pain and felt relieved. But then a few minutes later, the pain began and was intense. When I got home, I called one of my healers for advice. He said that I might be inflamed from the probe and recommended that I go to Cryotherapy. I headed straight there, and then went home to rest. I hoped that it would just be temporary soreness and not a major setback in my healing.

It's now been nearly a week since the colonoscopy, and the pain is still significantly worse than before the procedure. I don't know how much of a setback this is – how long the pain will continue to be this strong.

I feel crestfallen. After a year, I had finally felt close to the end, and now I feel further away. They didn't find any polyps and told me the results were good. I don't have to have a colonoscopy for another ten years. That's great news – although it does make me feel that the colonoscopy wasn't necessary and therefore may have been a mistake, since it intensified the pain. But I had no way of knowing in advance that the pain would be increased and there would be no polyps. As they say, hindsight is 20/20.

Yet, I have found some comfort in reading a book by a congregant of mine from Temple Har Shalom of Idyllwild named Kathy Harmon-Luber, who has struggled with chronic, debilitating pain for the past eight years. The book includes her powerful story as well as many meaningful quotes interspersed in the chapters. There are several quotes from her book that have struck me and that I've been thinking about a lot lately.

The first is by Perma Chodron saying, "Nothing goes away until it has taught us what we need to know."[50]

Rather than viewing the pain as a very unwanted guest, this quote suggests treating it instead as a teacher. The quote makes me wonder: what does the pain have left to teach me? Perhaps, it'll inspire me to take up yoga or to spend more time doing the relaxation audio from Dr. Wise or other types of meditation? Or who knows what else it has left to teach me?

What Pain Teaches Us

In Dr. Wise's workbook, I read that: "What we resist persists." Maybe, if I stop resisting the pain, it'll be more likely to go away.

One of my congregants from Open Temple, Rick, told me about a long health struggle that he faced and how a friend had suggested that he "redefine his relationship with pain." This idea proved to be crucial to his healing. He explained that when the pain came instead of panicking or wondering why this is happening to him, he instead simply said to himself: "This is what I am experiencing now."

In Buddhism, there's an idea of the second arrow – that when a person is shot by an arrow, we typically shoot ourselves with a second arrow – which is all the negative thoughts that go along with the fact that we've been shot by an arrow. Buddhism encourages avoiding injuring ourselves with the second arrow of upsetting thoughts.

Although my sufferings are not dear to me, and I want out of pain as soon as possible, if I view the pain as my teacher, I can wonder what it will teach me next. In fairness, although I passionately hate the pain, it has brought new people into my life who I admire and cherish, and it has taught me a great deal about human anatomy, healing, spirituality, and perseverance.

The second quote from Kathy's book which struck me is by Wendell Berry which says:

> *When we no longer know what to do, we have come to our real work, and when we no longer know which way to go, we have begun our real journey.*[51]

While the pain has taught me a great deal, in some ways it has left me dumfounded. There are parts of my life where I really don't know how to proceed – where I debate endlessly in my head what to do and it feels like I'm spinning my wheels and getting nowhere.

The Berry quote prompts me not to berate myself for not knowing what to do or which way to go – but rather to accept that this means I have real work ahead. I can only hope that the work and journey ahead will eventually lead to greater truth and more joy.

The Stranger

December 26, 2022

Are you a yoga instructor?" a lady asked me at the gym. I see her every morning between five and 6:30 AM, at the swimming pool, and we always wave hello, but we hadn't spoken before. I didn't know her name.

She explained that since she sees me do my stretches every morning, she thought that perhaps I am a yoga instructor.

"No," I answered, and I explained that I have an injury and am doing the stretches in hope of getting out of pain. She told me that she works at a physical therapy office and that many of the patients don't do the stretches that they are assigned, so she was impressed that I was doing the stretches every morning.

I was very grateful for the unexpected encouragement from this lady, and it lifted my spirits. Since she thought I looked like a Yoga instructor, I thought perhaps I should try a yoga class, so I did. I enjoyed the class. It felt like it was taking the stretching to the next level. I had been doing the same set of stretches from my doctors and healers for many months. The yoga class included some of these stretches but mostly offered new stretches which felt good.

A few weeks later, while at services at Open Temple, I overheard someone raving to a friend about Hot Yoga classes that she was taking, and I inquired to find out where she was taking them. I noticed that when I do my stretches in the sauna at the gym, I can reach further than when I do them outside the sauna. Since the heat of the sauna

Ilana Grinblat

helps with the stretches, I think that Hot Yoga could be good for me. I checked and the place that the person recommended for the Hot Yoga classes has a special for new students of one week of unlimited classes, so I plan to try that next week. I am appreciating how people who I don't even know are leading me in new, positive directions.

These conversations with strangers reminded me of the story of Joseph in the Bible. Torah portions of recent weeks tell the story of Joseph, whose rivalry with his brothers leads to them selling him into slavery in Egypt. While in Egypt, he ends up helping the Egyptian people through a famine. Before all this happens, the Torah which recounts the story of an unnamed man who Joseph asks where he can find his brothers and the man tells him where to find them.

This story is curious because it is unusual for the Torah to include any details that aren't crucial to the plot of the story. This episode of someone giving Joseph directions doesn't seem essential.

Commenting on this story, Rabbi Harold Kushner wrote:

> *We never hear of this man again. Yet if Joseph had not met him, he never would have found his brothers. He never would have been sold into slavery. The family would not have followed him into Egypt. There would have been no Exodus. The history of the world would have been so different! Could that man have known how his chance encounter changed history? Do we ever know the consequences of the little acts of thoughtfulness that we perform?*

When I think about my healing, I am struck by the number of people whose names I don't know who have helped. These people include the hospital transport workers, nursing assistants, clean-up crews and more.

At the gym, I enjoy seeing the same familiar faces each morning, and we've started to get to know each other. Every morning, I greet Blanca who cleans the sauna at 5:00 AM daily, and Gidon, an older gentleman who tells me each morning that he enjoys seeing my smiling face, and the lady (whose name I don't recall) who told me I looked like a yoga instructor. Each of them are part of my healing.

If I get into yoga, I'll have these anonymous strangers to thank for leading me to the next step in my healing. Regardless, I am grateful for the kindness of strangers throughout this journey.

On Worry

December 27, 2022

"How is it going with Jeremy away at college?" My friend, Roxana asked me on the phone.

"Okay," I told her truthfully. "I have much bigger problems to deal with."

For years, I had worried about what it would be like for me when Jeremy went away to college. My kids and I are very close. I couldn't imagine living in a different place than Jeremy (or Hannah for that matter) – and did not want to be apart from them on a regular basis. Prior to Jeremy going to college, I hadn't been apart from either child for longer than a week, and that week apart with them at scout camp, had only happened a couple times in each of their lives.

Whereas, I had worried about Jeremy going away to college, I had never worried that I would have a procedure that would leave me disabled and homebound. That idea had never crossed my mind. Luckily, Jeremy had gone to college about half an hour drive away from home, so I usually saw him each week. Even having Jeremy live in the dorms half an hour away was a big adjustment, but this change was *far* eclipsed by the bigger problems I have – the constant pain and all the ramifications that came along with losing my health, along with the ongoing struggle of trying to regain my strength and emerge from the prison of pain.

This interchange on the phone made me realize how futile worry is because I can't accurately anticipate what the future will look like. What

I think will be a big challenge, like adjusting to a child leaving for college, could easily be overshadowed by a bigger problem that I never saw coming. Whereas I did worry that the polyp would be cancerous (which it wasn't), I didn't worry that the procedure would go awry, and that nearly two years later, I would still be in constant agony. This prospect never occurred to me as a possibility.

In his book, *The Power of Now*, spiritual teacher Eckhart Tolle wrote about how useless worry is. He wrote that worry is "your mind which is projecting itself into an imaginary future situation and creating fear."[52]

He explained that:

> *There is no way that you can cope with such a situation because it doesn't exist. It's a mental phantom.*[53]

Tolle noted that worry is "a health and life-corroding insanity" which can be stopped by focusing on the present moment. He also wrote that one cannot handle any situation except in the present moment – in the now. He noted that:

> *You can always cope with the Now, but you can never cope with the future, nor do you have to. The answer, the strength, the right action, or the resource will be there when you need it, not before, not after.*[54]

This idea is reflected in the story of the Exodus. When the Israelites were preparing to flee from Egypt, Pharaoh offered that they could leave but would have to leave their flocks and herds behind. Moses rejected this offer saying that they needed to bring all their livestock along with them to choose which animals to bring as sacrifices. He explained: "We will not know with what we are to worship God until we come there."[55]

What Pain Teaches Us

Rabbi Harold Kushner applied this lesson to our own lives. He wrote:

> *God makes unique demands on each of us. We cannot know what God wants of us until we encounter God in each new stage of our lives.*[56]

This story serves to remind us not to get ahead of ourselves – that obsessing and worrying about the future is a futile exercise since the future is unknowable.

I received a painful reminder of this lesson while skiing. Hannah had wanted me to take her skiing, and even though I wasn't in good shape for skiing for the day, I figured I could do the easiest beginner slope, since that basically just involved standing and gliding gently down the hill. While riding on the ski lift to the beginner slope, I felt worried. One of my healers had injured his leg. He was going to the doctor the next day to find out if he had torn his ACL and would need surgery. I was worried for his health but also for my own because the surgery would mean that he wouldn't be able to help me for six months in order to recover.

As I was worrying about this idea, my ski got stuck in the snow on the mountain – since I hadn't lifted the tips of my skis up properly. One of my ski boots came off entirely, but the other ski was stuck and was twisting my ankle at a strange angle. I started screaming and crying, and the lift operator immediately stopped the lift. I removed the other ski and released my foot.

I then *really* had something to worry about. With a sprained ankle, I wouldn't be able to do my swimming and my stretches which were my recipe for healing. Thankfully, the ankle pain healed within a few days.

This moment was a powerful lesson. It was as if the universe was telling me, 'Don't worry about something that hasn't happened yet or I'll give you something real to worry about.' As it turns out, my healer hadn't torn his ACL and didn't need the surgery, but I had put myself

Ilana Grinblat

in danger and nearly sprained my ankle by worrying instead of paying attention.

Months later, I was worried about my losing my job. One of my healers pointed out to me that even though he had increased his expenses dramatically by renting a space for his new business, he wasn't worried about it.

"Do you know why I'm not worried?" he asked me.

"No, why?" I asked.

"Because worrying doesn't help," he said.

Once I realized the futility of worry, the question remained: how to stop. Old habits die hard.

The first step I took is no longer allowing myself to worry at night. If it was night and I was worried, I would ask myself rhetorically: Is the sun up or down? I would answer myself that the sun was down and then remind myself that I have plenty of time to worry about my problems all day, but at night, I have to rest. If I woke up at five A.M. and started worrying, I wouldn't allow myself to lie in bed stressing out and would get up and go to the gym instead.

During the day, I noticed how often I have difficult conversations in my mind with other people – imagining what they might say and how I would respond. When I noticed myself having such an internal dialogue, I would ask myself. 'Is that person here?' 'No,' I would answer internally. Then I would ask myself, 'then why are you talking to them?' I would remind myself of Eckhart Tolle's teaching that if I were having an actual conversation with this person, the right words with which to respond would come to me in the moment, not before and not after. No rehearsals are necessary.

What Pain Teaches Us

I also employed some tactics suggested in Dr. Lissa Rankin in *Mind over Medicine*. She cited a suggestion by meditation teacher Jack Kornfield that when meditating:

> *if you notice yourself remembering, planning or fantasizing, refrain from judging yourself, but do call it out.* "Hello, remembering," "Hello, planning," "Hello, fantasizing," *Then return to the present moment.*[57]

I employ this technique even when not meditating. When I notice myself thinking about worse case scenarios, I think "hello, catastrophizing," and then try to return to a more productive train of thought. I also remind myself that my body can't handle catastrophizing, so I can't live that way anymore.

Dr. Rankin also suggested using to a "thought-stopping technique" "to distract oneself from a pessimistic belief" with "attention shifting" wherein one "consciously concentrates on something else."[58] Based on this idea, when I find myself in a chain of thought that isn't useful, I instead learn a verse of Torah reading, starting from Genesis 1:1. I'm learning a lot of Torah this way!

I also try not to leave my mind unsupervised. I'll often watch videos of my favorite comedians so that rather than worrying, I'm laughing instead. As Milton Berle said, "Laughter is the best medicine in the world." Or as Bobby McFerrin sang, "Don't worry, be happy."

The Race

December 30, 2022

"I can't believe how limber you are," an older lady said to me at the gym. I appreciated her kind words of encouragement. I've been doing these stretches every day for over six months now. Still, it's hard for me to see my progress. The changes are so gradual and subtle, that they almost feel imperceptible.

Even though I have certainly become more limber, I still am in pain all day every day. I still lack the ability to sit without pain. Sitting is essential to functioning and interpersonal interaction. It's socially awkward to have a work lunch meeting where others are seated, and I am standing.

Especially now that we are on vacation, I feel this loss acutely. Yesterday, my family went to the movies, but I couldn't join them since sitting is still painful. Every meal becomes an issue – always checking out what type of seat is at each restaurant. Is it soft or hard? What is the angle of seat? Does it work to sit right now on this chair and if not, is there somewhere with a high counter where I can balance the plate and stand and eat? Standing for long stretches of time means that I get tired faster and typically fall asleep hours before the kids each night. There's no break or vacation from the pain.

"If this was something easy, we would have fixed it by now," one of my healers told me a while ago, and then listed some body parts that are easier to fix than this one, like a shoulder or an ankle. The truth is that the whole lower half of my body from fell apart – not just one part. "We want microwave solutions," my healer says. Our society

Ilana Grinblat

wants answers fast, just as the microwave heats food quickly. But with muscles, the work is slow and painstaking. As with love, muscles get stronger or weaker gradually over time.

"Give yourself a year," Dr. Wise had said at the workshop. It has been six and half months since he said those words to us. Still, over a year of pain has worn down my patience.

When I think about this slow progress, I think of stalagmites and stalactites and how the water carves through the rocks one drop at a time, incrementally over many years. Even though the rock seems much stronger than the water, the water does shape the rocks eventually.

This metaphor is also used in Jewish tradition for Torah study. According to a *midrash* (interpretation), a great sage named Rabbi Akiva was inspired to learn Torah from watching water drip on a rock. The text recounts:

> *What were Akiva's beginnings? It is said: Up to the age of forty, he had not yet studied a thing. One time, while standing by the mouth of a well in Lydda, he inquired, "Who hollowed out this stone?" and was told, "Akiva, haven't you read that 'water wears away stone'* [59] *(Job 14:19)? - it was water falling upon it constantly, day after day." At that, Rabbi Akiva asked himself: Is my mind harder than this stone? I will go and study at least one section of Torah.*[60]

This moment marked a turning point in Rabbi Akiva's life. "He went on to become the greatest sage on his generation, with 24,000 student learning under him at one time."[61]

Perhaps, like Torah study, healing too comes drop by drop, bit by tiny bit. But perhaps, if the steady drop of water can carve a well, and Rabbi Akiva can go from not knowing the Hebrew alphabet to become the greatest scholar of his generation, then I will someday be out of pain. As the saying goes: "slow and steady wins the race."

In Between

January 2, 2023

"Are you able to go bowling with us today?" Jeremy asked me while we were on winter vacation in Nevada.

"I have no idea." I told him honestly.

My pain level has been so variable lately. I have made progress. I can drive a car with the aid of an infrared light pad, and I am getting more limber in my stretches. But the pain can act up at any time with no warning.

It's a strange time. I have no idea from moment to moment what I am or am not capable of. I am in between sick and well – in between being entirely debilitated and being capable and independent. While I'm grateful for the progress, I hate this feeling of in between and all the not knowing that it entails.

I've never been good at transitions. I'm better with black and white – not so good with all the shades of gray in between. I'm better with clear categories and divisions than with the messiness of not fitting into any box.

This time feels like an emotional rollercoaster. When I feel better, I get excited and want to try activities that I love and haven't been able to do in a long time – like skiing or ice skating – but then when the pain intensifies, I become crestfallen. Somehow, it feels even worse to feel restricted again when I thought I was almost out of pain.

Ilana Grinblat

There is a saying in Jewish tradition for how I've been feeling. The Hebrew phrase for being in between is *bein hashemashot* (which means between the suns). In rabbinic literature, this term is used for the transitional times of day – sunset and sunrise – the times that are neither day nor night. Whereas these times of day defy neat categories, the rabbis teach that *bein hashemashot* is a time when miracles happen.

According to the rabbis, there are ten special things that were created at twilight on the cusp of the first Sabbath of creation. They were:

> *the mouth of the earth (which swallowed Korach), the mouth of the well (of Miriam, that provided water for the Israelites in the desert); the mouth of the donkey (Balaam's talking donkey); the rainbow; the manna; the staff (Moses'); the* shamir *(the worm that cut the stones of the Altar in the Holy Temple); and the writing, the inscription and the tablets (of the Ten Commandments).*[62]

These extraordinary occurrences defy categorization and break down divisions. For example, the talking donkey of the Balaam story in the Book of Numbers breaks down the separation between animals (which normally can't speak in words) and humans. These things remind us that the world is not so easily separated into clear-cut categories. Somehow, the toughest times of life – the narrow times – remind us that life is more complex and nuanced than it seems.

Many items on this list involve communication. The first three on the list refer to the "mouth," and the last three on the list relate to writing. Somehow, the narrow times are often also the times of greatest creativity. I am writing more now than before this illness, and I am surely not alone. Many of the most powerful books I've read have come out of major crises in the life of their authors.

Several things on the list provided sustenance on difficult journeys. The mouth of the well of Miriam gave water to the Israelites through their arduous desert trek to the Promised Land. The mouth of the donkey told Balaam that there was an angel on the path before him that he hadn't seen.

I am also struck by the image of the mouth of the earth that swallowed up the priest Korach and his followers after they rebelled against Moses (as recounted in the book of Numbers). Indeed, part of me feels restless and rebellious nowadays. I feel like kicking down the walls of restriction that have held me in for so long. I feel like Rapunzel, eager to flee from the tower where she's been held captive for so long.

This time has also felt to me like a series of earthquakes. Sometimes, this time feels so overwhelming that I feel like I might get swallowed up into the ground like Korach and his followers. The despair threatens to engulf me completely. I want to curl up on the ground and not get up again. Through these earthquakes, many of the assumptions that I previously took as a given have crumbled beneath my feet. Life is more far more complicated than I realized, and sadly, so am I.

As much as I hate being in this state of *bein hashemashot*, I appreciate that this is a time where great miracles and where angels have come into my life. As I bowl and write these words with the snow falling outside the window, I hope someday to emerge from the confinement of pain and say:

Min hametzar karati yah, anani b'merchav yah: From the narrow place I called to you, God, and you answered me with divine wide-open expanse."[63]

What Do You Need?

January 13, 2023

I was talking with Idan, Open Temple's musician in residence, who has suffered with chronic pain for eighteen years. He recommended a technique that he does to help him with the pain. While lying down, he puts his hand on the painful area, and says, "What do you need?" The area then tends to move and shift to a better position. He recommends doing this for fifteen minutes.

Rather than thinking of the pain as the enemy, he recommends treating it with loving-kindness in this way, as you would a lover. When a romantic partner expresses frustration, a helpful approach is to ask gently: What is going on? What does this person need? Likewise, the pain is expressing frustration, so we lovingly ask it what it needs and give it the time to get what it needs.

This reminds me again of the story in Genesis about Abraham's maidservant Hagar. When she ran out of food and water in the desert and lost hope, an angel of God appeared and said, *Mah lach Hagar*, which means literally, "What is to you, Hagar" The angel asked her what she needed. After this interchange, Hagar saw a well of water in front of her that she hadn't noticed previously because of her despair.

Indeed, Idan's technique was helpful. When I put my hand on the painful area and asked the pain, "what do you need?" I too found that the muscles would start to adjust to a more comfortable position. Idan's approach reminded me to treat my pain – and more broadly my wounded heart with tenderness and love, rather than frustration.

In the summary of his home program for pelvic pain, Dr. David Wise recounted an old fable about the sun and north wind arguing about who was more powerful. In this story, the sun and the wind engaged in a contest to see who could prompt a man walking on earth to take off his jacket first.

According to this tale:

> *The north wind went first. He blew and blew on the man, and the man held onto his jacket more and more tightly. When the north wind exhausted himself as the man stubbornly held onto his jacket he gave up and told the sun it was his turn. And the sun shone on the man, more and more brightly and warmly, until the man took off his jacket. The sun won the contest.*[64]

Dr. Wise applied this parable to the relaxation technique that he teaches, saying:

> *In your relaxation practice, we are asking you to be the sun shining on that stubborn part of you that won't take off its "jacket." We bring sunshine, warmth, friendship, non-judgment, and respect to the part of us that is closed and contracted.*[65]

A week after Idan told me his technique for addressing pain, I attended a Friday night service at Open Temple. During the service, Rabbi Lori Shapiro called for those who were sick or were praying for a sick loved one to come down to her and form a circle with her, embracing one another. Idan and the band played a melody that he had composed to the prayer, "*El Na Refana la*" (which means God, please heal her). This prayer is the words that Moses said when his sister Miriam was sick."[66] The chant repeated over and over, getting faster and more powerful with each incantation. The beat pounded stronger, and our voices raised louder with each repetition.

El Na Refana La.

El Na Refana La.

"*El Na Refana Ilana,*" Rabbi Lori said to me.

I closed my eyes. I felt Rabbi Lori's arm around my waist on one side and Tal's arm around me on the other side. Over and over, I chanted the prayer for myself and for Idan and all those in need of healing. I felt strengthened by the support of Jeremy who was operating the projector in the booth, Hannah who was watching from the front row, and the whole community all singing together in unison.

I felt a slight shift in my left buttock, which diminished the pain in that area.

I was exhausted. I was struggling, but I was determined, and I wasn't alone.

Perhaps the sun would come out tomorrow after all.

Good Days and Bad Days

January 31, 2023

It was January 31st. My pain level was lower than usual. My hopes soared. Maybe, just maybe, I thought, my healer was right.

He had said a few months earlier that if I kept up doing what I was doing (the daily stretches and swimming, and weekly massages), then he thought I could be out of pain in January. At first, I'd hoped that I could beat his estimate. But as December wore on and the pain continued, I realized that wouldn't be the case. At least, I hoped I could reach his estimate and be out of pain in January. When I felt better than usual on January 31st, I was encouraged. But then February 1st came, and the pain was worse than it had been the day before. My hopes plummeted.

Each day feels like an emotional roller-coaster. When the pain lessens, my spirits lift, but then the pain gets worse, and my hopes are dashed again. During my stretches at the gym, I feel the muscles loosen up and think: 'Something good is happening.' 'I'm getting somewhere,' 'I'm going to get out of pain.' But then an hour later, the pain increases and along with it, melancholy returns to my heart. After thirteen months of this, I am emotionally exhausted. When the pain lessens, I don't want to get my hopes up too high, fearing they will crash again. I guard myself against feeling joy when the pain eases, reluctant to trust the improvement. But whether I let my hopes go up or not, I always end up feeling sad. I can't win.

I explained to one of my healers how my emotions were going up and down with the pain every day like a roller coaster. "You can't do that," he said. "This is how it's going to be now. You're going to have good days and bad days. But remember where you were a year ago. Remember where you were six months ago. Remember how far you've come."

Although my healers see my progress, I have trouble recognizing it. All I feel is that I am still in pain at every moment.

Somehow, even though I know the pain is getting less, the longer this goes on, the harder it is becoming emotionally. I am somehow getting physically better but emotionally worse. I am searching for a "Happily Ever After" Ending. I am imagining that at a significant date, this nightmare will end. Perhaps, it would be at the one year-anniversary of the surgery. Perhaps a Hanukkah miracle. Perhaps in January, as one of my healers had estimated. Perhaps in June, the one-year anniversary of the pelvic pain workshop. But these dates come and go, and the pain remains. I picture the pain as prison, from which one day, the door will open, and I will run out into the open air – elated and finally free. But it isn't so simple. There is no easy pill or magic bullet. The recipe for healing can't been heated quickly in the microwave – only prepared in the slow cooker. Pain is powerful and complex; it eludes any clear answers.

Sometimes, I wish for an external/objective scale on which the pain could be measured, which would give me a number. Then I could see, last week, I was at a fifty, and this week, I'm at a forty, and I would be able to see my progress. When my father asks me what percentage I am compared to normal, I could answer him accurately. When it comes to pain, I felt like I am either in it or out of it, but I can't quantify it. I could see only black and white -- not the shades of gray.

My healers are pleased with my progress, but I can't see it. Just as Hagar couldn't see the well of water before her until the angel pointed it out to her, I too have trouble recognizing my improvement until someone reminds me of it.

One of my healers said, "I know that the way into the pain was very fast, but the way out is going to be very slow." This statement reminded me about a verse about the story of the Exodus from slavery in Egypt which says:

> *Now when Pharaoh let the people go, God did not lead them by way of the land of the Philistines because it was closer, for God said, "The people might have a change of heart when they see war and return to Egypt."*[67]

When fleeing slavery in Egypt, God didn't take the Israelite people on a direct route, although it was shorter but instead chose an indirect route, even though it was longer.

This verse always puzzled me. One would think that when fleeing oppression, one would want to take the quickest route possible, especially if Pharaoh's army is chasing after you!

Some commentators offer practical reasons for the indirect route. One commentator named Minhah B'lulah said that God was trying to avoid the possibility of the Israelites being attacked by the Philistines on the way if they went by the more direct route. Other commentators suggest that the longer route would allow the Israelites more time to develop the determination they would need when they enter the Promised Land.

Still, others offer a more spiritual explanation – noting that sometimes in life, the longer path is preferable. In the Talmud, a rabbi named Yehoshua ben Haninyah recounted the following story:

> *One time I was walking along the path, and I saw a young boy sitting at the crossroads. And I said to him: On what path shall we walk to the city? He said to me: This path is short and long, and that path is long and short. I walked on the path that was short and long. When I approached the city, I found that gardens and orchards blocking the path.*
>
> *I went back and said to the boy: "My son, didn't you tell me that this way is short?"*
>
> *He said to me: "And didn't I tell you that it is also long?"*
>
> *I kissed him and said to him: "Happy are you, O Israel, for you are all exceedingly wise, from your old to your young."*[68]

In reflecting on this story, I am struck by the image of two paths, "a short way which is long and a long way which is short."[69] These paths seem emblematic of two different approaches to healing.

In my experience, the path of Western medicine has been "the short way which is long." Western medicine seems to offer faster solutions to the pain – such as a pill, surgery, or nerve block procedure. But this path is longer than it seems. The pills and the procedures reduce the pain, but they also take away my strength which takes me a long time to get back. While these approaches appear initially to remove the pain, this shortcut is an illusion. As Rabbi Leder wrote of his experience with pills, "the pain was dulled but the pain was still in charge."[70] With pills, I'm also particularly terrified of getting caught in the thicket of addiction from which to extricate oneself takes a very long time.

By contrast, the path of Eastern medicine -- of stretches, muscle massage, relaxation, yoga, etc. seems like the long way. It takes hours a day of hard work over long stretches of time. The improvement is so gradual that it can be barely noticeable from day to day. But ultimately, this circuitous path may be the shortest. This path doesn't rob me of my strength. Instead, it builds my endurance, fosters my determination and resilience, and leads me to a more spiritual, deeper way of living.

Certainly, I wish that my way out of pain had been as short as my way in. If so, I would have felt better the next day after the surgery, but alas, this wasn't the case. I try to remind myself that like it or not, just like the way out of Egypt, my way out of pain is the indirect route.

Like the Exodus, the path out of pain is slow and painstaking. The muscles need to be gently coaxed, bit by bit every day until they loosen up and let go.

With muscles and with relationships, often progress can only be measured in long time frames. I overheard Rabbi Lori on the phone talking with a man who recently divorced and who was struggling with his relationship with his daughter. She advised, "instead of thinking in years, you need to think in decades." She told him that fixing his relationship with his estranged daughter will be a long-term project. He shouldn't measure the improvement in that relationship in days, months or even years but instead over decades.

Every couple of months on Friday night at Open Temple, we have a service called Kirtan Shabbat which is inspired by Indian chanting. As I sat down on the floor in the front row, I remembered how I felt a couple months prior when this service was last held. At that previous service, I couldn't sit down at all and had to stand in the back the whole time. At this service, I was able to sit on the floor – though I couldn't yet sit in a chair. Although I can't see my progress in my health from day to day, I can see it over the span of months.

At that service, like Hagar opening her eyes to the well of water in front of her, I got a glimpse of my improvement which sustained me on my journey through the desert of pain. While I still wish for a swifter exit from pain, I can only hope that like the Israelites, I'm learning valuable lessons on this slow, indirect route.

Unlocking the Gate

May 13, 2023

At the gym, I often have trouble unlocking my combination lock. I keep making the same mistake. I turn it in the proper directions to the correct numbers, but the lock still stays shut. The reason is that I forget to pause at the numbers in the code.

At a baby naming for Open Temple, I shared the idea of the gym locker as a metaphor for our lives. We often run from one task to another, doing everything we're supposed to do, but we forget to pause and to absorb the majesty of any given moment – and therefore our hearts stay locked.

This baby naming was on a spring Saturday morning, so I suggested that the Sabbath offers us a time to pause and to unlock the gates to our hearts. I also shared a story from the Maggid of Dubno, an eighteenth-century storyteller from Lithuania, about how to unlock gates.

> *Once there was a father who traveled with his son for miles. Each time they reached an obstacle such as a river or mountain, the father lifted his son on his shoulders and carried him through the difficult terrain. Finally, they came to their destination—a walled castle. But the gate of the castle was shut, and there were only narrow windows on the sides of the wall.*
>
> *The father said to his son; "My son, up until now I have carried you. Now the only way we can reach our destination is if you will climb through the windows and open the gate for me from within."*

> *So, it is... with parents and children and God. Parents take care of their children, feed and clothe them, and see them through all sorts of obstacles. Yet parents, who have so many strengths, often find the gate to God closed. But children have a special spiritual magic. They can climb to places their parents cannot reach. Children fling open the gates of heaven from within so that they and their parents can reach God together.*[71]

While this story is about parents and children, it also contains an important lesson for all of us. The gates to God can only be unlocked from within – from inside us. Breaking down the barriers to spirituality is an inside job, one that requires a long journey.

Before the baby naming, I had taken a walk with Lori and shared with her the struggles that I had been having with my medical crisis and the impact it was having on my life. After the baby naming, Rabbi Lori Shapiro said to me: "You know that speech you gave was intended for you. All you need to do now is stop."

That night, I slept fourteen hours. It was the first time I had slept well for as long as I could remember. Just being heard and seen by Lori had made a big difference. At least for that night, my body followed Rabbi Lori's orders and stopped for a rest.

For the last seventeen months, my response to my medical crisis has been running. I've run to doctors, hospitals, massage therapists, cryotherapy, the gym, and other treatments. I ran to my jobs. I left one job due to my medical problems -- only to end up with four new part-time jobs. I also ran to be there for my kids and other familial responsibilities. The more I ran, the more I became run down. The one thing I haven't done is pause.

A year ago, the program Dr. Wise prescribed at the pelvic pain workshop contained several components – stretches, internal and external trigger point devices, reading, videos, and a relaxation audio exercise. I did it all – with gusto – except the relaxation component with which I really struggled. The program calls for 2-3 hours per day of lying down and listening to the relaxation audio recordings. That part I haven't done much.

What Pain Teaches Us

A few weeks later, I ended up following Lori's advice to stop – not on purpose, but against my will. One of my healers had recommended that I go back to the doctors. After thirteen months, my progress had plateaued. Despite many, many daily stretches, there were a couple crucial spots at the juncture of my legs and my pelvis that were still unrelentingly painful every waking moment. I was reluctant to return to the doctors since they had been stumped before and had advised all sorts of treatments that didn't work, but my healer insisted it was time. So, I went.

First, I went to the general doctor, who sent me to the dermatologist to fix a bump in the area. The dermatologist fixed the bump but said it wasn't the source of the pain and sent me to the neurologist. The neurologist suggested that I take a medicine called Cymbalta which she had prescribed to me four months prior, but I had been too scared to take. The medicine was both a treatment for nerve pain as well as an antidepressant. I reluctantly tried the medicine. At first, I was supposed to take one pill, then if I tolerated the medicine, I was instructed to take two pills, and then if tolerating the increased dose, I was expected to increase to three pills per day which is the intended dosage.

I took one pill per day for two weeks. The pill diminished the pain somewhat and made me feel lightheaded. I had trouble concentrating, driving, and sleeping. After two weeks, I started taking two pills a day which took away the pain almost entirely, but I had even more trouble driving, sleeping, and concentrating. After five days on two pills, I ended up lying down on the floor outside the bathroom at work unable to talk, think, and walk. Lori said it was time to go to the hospital, and my stepmother Melissa came to take me.

Fortunately, while waiting to be admitted to the hospital, the effects of the medicine which I had taken the previous night began to wear off. Melissa drove me home where over the next week, I weaned myself off the medicine and regained the ability to think, speak, and walk – and regained my strength.

Dr. Gabor Mate, a physician, author, and filmmaker who has devoted his life to studying trauma wrote that:

Ilana Grinblat

> *If you don't know how to say 'no' when you need to, your body will say it for you in the form of illness.*[72]

For the prior eighteen months of my illness, I hadn't said no. I had tried through my illness to keep going, but now I had to stop. At Lori's suggestion, I went on medical leave again for the summer. I charged the iPad which contained the relaxation audio and resolved that this time, I will add that to my daily regimen. I hope that by stopping, I'll unlock the gate to the prison of pain and go free – and perhaps also unlock the gates to my heart and soul.

My Birthday Present

June 2, 2023

My dad and stepmom invited our family over for Shabbat dinner in honor of my fiftieth birthday which was coming up the next week. But eighteen-months into this medical crisis, I could not imagine feeling any less like celebrating. The day before had been a breaking point for me. I had been crying off and on most of the day. I looked like hell. I knew that if I walked through the door of my folks' home, they would take one look at me and be worried. I literally did not have the strength to put on a happy face and pretend to be cheery for my birthday celebration.

On the way home from work, I called their home and Melissa answered. "I can come for dinner tonight, but don't make me pretend to be okay."

"Just come and let us feed you," she said, "let us care for you."

Somehow, that phone call took the pressure off. I didn't have to put on a brave face anymore. And the tone and tenor of the evening had changed in ways I can't quite put into words. The air seemed a bit lighter. I laughed more than I had at previous dinners at their home.

Knowing how I was feeling, my dad took me aside to the other room to talk. In that conversation, I brought up to him the tragic story of Rabbi Steven Tucker, of blessed memory. Rabbi Tucker was a wonderful, highly esteemed rabbi in the Los Angeles Jewish community, who had been president of the region of the Rabbinical Assembly. Whenever I saw him, he was cheery and schmoozy. He had a beautiful family – a wife and three wonderful children. But then he faced a personal crisis, his congregation didn't renew his contract, and he took his car in the middle of the night and drove himself off a cliff and died.

"What was Rabbi Tucker supposed to do?" I asked my dad.

"Talk to someone," he answered, "a rabbi, or a therapist." My dad invited me back for a walk the next day after services to talk more.

On Saturday morning, I went to a bar mitzvah – which was the most moving bar mitzvah I've ever attended. It was the bar mitzvah of a thirty-eight-year-old man, Zach Richter, who is on the board of Open Temple. Zach had been asked by his dad at age twelve if he wanted to have a bar mitzvah, but he declined because he was worried about learning the material in time. Over the years, Zach came to feel that he had missed out by not have a bar mitzvah and once he had a son, he felt eager to have his bar mitzvah both for himself and to model for his son the importance of Jewish tradition.

That morning, I was visibly shaken. "Are you okay?" Zach asked. "No, I said, "but I'm grateful to be here with you." Somehow, telling the truth again felt like a relief. I didn't have to deny any part of my experience. I could convey both parts at once – both how "not okay" I was and yet at the same time, how glad I was to be there.

Before the service began, music was playing for the attendees as they gathered. The song was "Anthem" by Leonard Cohen. The lyric was:

> *There is a crack, a crack in everything*
> *That's how the light gets in.*

"This song is for you." Lori said to me.

By the time my birthday rolled around – a week later, I was *much* more "not okay" than I had been at Zach's bar mitzvah. The medication was wreaking havoc on my body and mind. After the bar mitzvah, I went on a walk with my father but that was the last time I could walk without dizziness. That night, I had tried to walk to my car to go home, and I couldn't do it. "You're not going anywhere," my folks said, I spent the night attempting (and failing) to sleep in their guesthouse.

Sunday night, I spent the night failing to sleep in my office since I didn't think that I could drive to work and wanted to teach my classes the next day. Instead of teaching, I ended up lying on the floor at work, coming in and out of consciousness. For the next week, as I weaned myself off the medicine, my abilities to walk, think, talk, and sleep and came and went. It was the most terrifying week of my life.

For my birthday, I couldn't go out to dinner – since I couldn't walk.

One of my healers had told me that when I get light-headed, I should eat protein. So, I had the kids cook a bunch of chicken for me to eat to regain my strength. On my birthday, Hannah brought me a piece of chicken with a candle burning in it and told me to make a wish. I made a wish and blew out the candle. "I know what you wished for," she said. She knew without asking that I had wished for health.

While I wished for health, what I got for my birthday was truth. My birthday present was not having to pretend anymore that I was okay in any way, shape, or form. At least, that weight was lifted. It wasn't the gift I wanted, but it was the one I desperately needed.

In the days leading up to and all around my birthday, I started saying painful truths that I had been avoiding for a long time. Sometimes, it didn't feel like a good trade. "Maybe, pretending was better," I told Tal.

When the choice is between ugly, excruciating truth and pretty lies, it's a tough call. Sometimes, lying for the sake of *shalom bayit* (peace in the house) seems better. Even our tradition says that it's ok to lie for the sake of avoiding hurt feelings. The Talmud notes that it is preferable to tell a bride on her wedding day that she's beautiful, regardless of whether you think she's pretty or not.[73]

Over time, however, lies can build up and become heavy. It takes too much strength to carry them anymore. Like plaque, the lies build up and corrode whatever they touch.

"Sometimes we have to hear the truth, even when it's painful." a friend told me, "People have given their lives so that you can speak your truth. Speak your truth."

This idea reminded me of a story about the creation of humanity. Genesis recounts that before creating humanity, God said, "Let us make people in our image, after our likeness."[74] Who is the "us" in this sentence? Since Judaism believes that there are no other gods and humans and animals hadn't been created yet, who was God talking to?

The rabbis explained that God was speaking to the angels, consulting with them about the idea of creating humanity. According to a rabbinic legend, the angels had a vigorous debate among themselves as to whether creating people was a good idea or not. The angel of lovingkindness said it was a good idea to create humanity because people will do many acts of kindness. The angel of truth advised God not to create human beings because they will be full of lies. The angel of justice recommended in favor of creating humanity because they will pursue justice, but the angel of peace opposed creating people because they will make much violence.[75]

The angel advisors were tied two to two. The jury was deadlocked. So, how could God decide whether to create humanity or not? According to the story, God knocked the angel of truth down to the ground, which is proven using the Biblical verse, "truth springs up from the ground."[76]

This legend says a great deal about truth. You can push truth down, shove it under the rug over and over, but no matter how many times you knock it down, somehow it springs back up again. Whether one tells lies of omission or commission, lying is like a giant game of Whac-A-Mole that you can never win. The truth will just keep bouncing back up again until you're simply too tired to hammer it down anymore.

I did get some presents for my birthday – a season pass to Hurricane Harbor (the local water park) and a gift certificate to a spa called Glen Ivy. I am not healthy enough to use either of these gifts but pray to gain the strength to use them soon.

The only gift that I got for my birthday that I can use right now is the truth. The sad truth is that I'm not okay at all. Nonetheless, I am still grateful to be here and am entirely unwilling to drive myself over any cliffs. The truth of the havoc that my medical condition has wrought on my life is ugly and brutally painful. In many senses, pretending to be okay – to have the perfect life – was prettier and more peaceful. But the truth kept springing up from the ground until I didn't have the strength to fight it anymore. The truth wore me down. When I fought against truth, I won some battles but lost the war.

What I got for my fiftieth birthday was being defeated by the angel of truth. In our wrestling match, the angel of truth pinned me down to the ground until I admitted that I was shattered and splintered into many pieces.

This loss made me think of a passage from the Talmud. The rabbis asked what should be done if there is a house which is built with a stolen beam in its foundation. One group of rabbis called the House of Shammai argued that the house must be torn down, and the stolen beam returned to its owner. A second group of rabbis called the House of Hillel said that the value of the stolen beam should be returned to the owner, but the house can stay standing.[77]

On my fiftieth birthday, the house that I had built -- which had a beam which was a lie – collapsed. I don't know how to rebuild from here. But whatever I do build from here will have to be built on a foundation of truth – ugly, brutal *emet* – my truth.

Also in the Talmud, a rabbi named Yirmiyah asked whether a priest can officiate the religious rites if his body is inside the tabernacle, but his head is outside. A rabbi named Zera answered no. He explained that the whole priest has to be in the tent including his head. Only if he put his entire self into the tabernacle could he officiate.[78]

Like the priest, I had to admit the truth that my body, mind, heart, and soul are in all different places – and I can't go on that way anymore. I need all the pieces of me in one place. Like Humpty Dumpty, I have fallen off the wall and now must pick up all the broken pieces of me and try to put them back together again.

"When everything falls apart, something new is about to be born," Lori told me. "There's nothing more traumatic than being born through a birth canal," she explained. Indeed, in In Hebrew, the word for crisis – *Mashber* – is also the word for birth stool. In childbirth, only by contracting can we expand. So too in life. As Rabbi Steve Leder wrote, "the truth is that most often for most people, real growth comes from real pain."[79]

"You're having an awakening," Lori told me. (Perhaps that can explain why I can't sleep!)

I hope that the song lyric and Rabbis Lori and Steve are right. I hope that there will be light that comes through all this brokenness. As I fall apart, I pray that something new is about to be born, and that all this pain will lead to growth. That's my real birthday wish.

Too Tight

July 3, 2023

"You're strumming too hard," Hannah told me. I recently learned to play guitar and was practicing leading prayers. Hannah pointed out to me that if I strummed more gently then it would sound better. I tried it, and she was right. In addition to strumming to hard, I notice that I was also holding the guitar too tightly. When I loosened my grip on the guitar, the music sounded better.

I realized at that moment that Hannah's point wasn't limited to the guitar. I was grasping much of life too tightly. Perhaps, my pain was a physical manifestation of a deeper problem, of holding on too hard to the stresses of life.

Recently, a congregant told me that hearing about my medical problems reminded him of the story of Job in the bible. I figured if he's right, then perhaps I should study the book of Job. There, I was struck by the phrase "girding one's loins."

In the Bible, the phrase "girding your loins" refers to preparing for battle. In biblical times, the common clothing was a tunic. Girding one's loins means rolling up a tunic and tucking under a belt or tying it in a knot to attain greater freedom of movement in preparation for war, a long journey, running, or hard labor.[80]

This phrase is also associated with serious illness. The book of Job recounts that Satan afflicted "a severe inflammation on Job from the sole of his foot to the crown of his head."[81] In agony and despair, Job cried out to God – cursing the day he was born. God spoke to him out of the whirlwind and told him to "gird his loins like a man."[82] God reminded Job that he wasn't there when God created the earth. God reminded Job of God's great power and Job's lack thereof.

The phrase, "girding one's loins" represents the idea that one must tighten the area of one's loins to be ready to respond to a situation in which one feels powerless and anxious. Pelvic pain may be the body's attempt to girds its loins – tightening the pelvic muscles in response to crisis. Yet, over time this constant tightening can have devastating consequences. Chronic tightening of the pelvic muscles causes more pain and therefore more stress in a self-perpetuating cycle.

In his workbook on pelvic pain, Dr. Wise discussed the view that often to feel safe in life, we think that "the only way to protect myself is to stay guarded an alert."[83] Dr. Wise noted that paradoxically, it's actually the letting go of this hyper vigilance that is the gateway to safety and peace.

What is the opposite of vigilance? Joy.

Rabbi Menachem Mendel of Zotzk of eighteenth/nineteenth century Poland said, "It is a great mitzvah (commandment) to be happy at all times." This statement always puzzled me. With all the pain of life, how can one possibly be happy at all times? Perhaps, Rabbi Menachem Mendel was pointing toward an aspiration – nudging us to experience the lightness that comes from letting go of vigilance.

Rabbi Menachem Mendel's words echoed to me through more contemporary voices in my life. As one of my healers said, "Life is meant to be enjoyed." Or as Hannah reminds me, "Mom, you're strumming too hard."

The Road Less Travelled

July 12, 2023

As a gift, my boss and dear friend, Rabbi Lori Shapiro, gave me a treatment at an Ayurveda spa. (Ayurveda is a type of traditional medicine from India).I had no idea what to expect -- except that I suspected it would be weird.

And weird it was.

As I reviewed the preparatory instructions that the spa provided, I knew I was in uncharted territory. For the first four of the five days before the treatment, I had to begin the day by heating and then ingesting a substance called ghee -- two teaspoons of melted ghee on the first morning, then doubling the quantity on each of the three subsequent days. I have no idea what was in ghee, but before melting it was a consistency I don't normally associate with food, more like with rubber. The instructions specified that the ghee might make you feel nauseous -- which it did.

During the five days before the treatment, I was only allowed to eat specific foods -- dishes I'd never heard of. I could buy the food or make it myself. The ingredients list to prepare these dishes contained items I didn't recognize and had no idea where to buy. I was clearly out of my league and decided to buy the food. The spa staff told me that the director of the spa, doesn't believe in leftovers, so I should come each day at noon to get the food for the next twenty for hours. The canisters of food were very small -- certainly not enough to feel satisfied. 'I guess I'm on a diet now,' I thought.

Ilana Grinblat

On the fifth day, I had to ingest two tablespoons of castor oil in the morning and depending on how many bowels movements I had, I would then be allowed to eat the prepared food for the rest of the day. (If I had too many bowel movements, then I'd have to be on a liquid diet that day.) Luckily, I had the right number of bowel movements and was therefore allowed to eat the small quantities of unrecognizable foods. I'd never been so delighted to have a specified number of bowel movements!

During the five days of preparation, there were also additional restrictions – no sex or exercise. Even taking a nap wasn't allowed. I followed the instructions diligently – but wondered: What were they trying to do to me? I felt tired from the lack of food, but then wasn't even allowed to nap. When I got sleepy and told Jeremy that I wasn't allowed to nap, he said that there are no napping police that would arrest me if I slept. But still, if I was going to do this, I would do it all the way – so I stayed awake.

When I finished the five days preparation, I was feeling weak and light-headed. I came to the treatment with absolutely no idea what to expect. When I got there, I asked about the plan for the day, but even the people who worked there couldn't tell me what would happen. They told me that the director specially designs each person's treatment based on their medical condition, so they don't know what to do until the director tells them.

Each day, the treatment began with two people doing a massage on me with lots of oil. That was normal enough. Then the treatments got stranger from there. One day, there was a warm to sit pot to sit out for a vaginal steam. Another day, bags of very hot rice and milk that were tapped on my body – covering me in milky slime – apparently designed somehow to cool my body from the inside out. Each day ended with a different type of enema that had to be held in for a different amount of time before releasing it – and then hot oil poured on my forehead for a while, until my hair was dripping with oil – all the while with Indian chants playing in the background. All these things had funky Indian names to them.

What Pain Teaches Us

Yet after the initial oil massage and before the other treatments came what was for me the most powerful and transformative times. Each day a neuro-muscular massage therapist worked with me and gave me crucial insights about my medical condition and how to treat it.

Those insights though weren't easy. Rather, these massages were very painful – both physically and emotionally.

The first day, an incredible neuro-muscular massage therapist named Lisa worked with me. She asked me all about my medical history – especially as related to my pelvic area. I told her that after my son was born nineteen years ago, the placenta didn't come out like it was supposed to, and so the doctor used her hands to remove my uterus through my vagina and take out the placenta from my uterus and then put the uterus back in. I also told her about my second pregnancy and delivery (which thankfully was normal) and then my third pregnancy which ended in miscarriage and then the polyp removal, nineteen months ago which left me in pain ever since. I told her about the treatments I've tried over the past nineteen months for the pain – the four nerve block procedures, seven bladder procedures, hospital stays, the acupuncture, massage therapy, medications, etc.

She told me that when my uterus was removed during Jeremy's delivery, the uterus was severed from my sacrum (which it is supposed to be connected to) and therefore I have scar tissue. She said that the culmination of the first pregnancy and delivery with its complications, the second pregnancy and delivery, the third pregnancy and miscarriage, and then the polyp removal was too much for my body which couldn't take it anymore.

I started crying. I had no idea that I had damage from Jeremy's delivery nineteen years ago. My mind filled with questions: Why hadn't the doctor told me about this? Was there any way the placenta could have been removed without severing my uterus from my sacrum?

I knew that the polyp removal had gone awry nineteen months ago. I feel that the removal should have been done under anesthesia so that my muscles wouldn't have all contracted due to the pain of the procedure – leaving me in pain for the last 19 months. So that was one medical mistake that I knew about – but I had no idea that 19 years prior, another medical mistake had happened to me that I was still suffering all these years later without even knowing about it.

As I cried, Lisa gently asked me about what I was feeling, and I told her. She shared that she had a car accident years earlier that she has to go to physical therapy for every week for the rest of her life. She explained though that she doesn't feel resentment or regret about the car accident. She noted that since we can't change anything that happens to us in life, we just need to accept it as part of our healing journey. She explained that caring for one's health is an investment in ourselves.

"You're being very brave," she said, "because you've chosen to take the path of healing – which is harder." She noted how diligently I'd been trying in both Western and Eastern medicine to heal.

"There's no other choice," I told her. "I have to do everything I can to get out of this pain."

"No," she said, "there is another choice. Many people do nothing and just continue to be in pain – because that's the easier path. But you have chosen the path of healing. That is a harder path, and you have been brave to have chosen that path."

Her statement reminded me of a quote by Napolean Bonaparte who said, "Bravery isn't having the strength to go on. It's going on when you don't have strength."

As I drove to the spa each day, I listened to a course about Ayurvedic healing taught by my congregant and friend Kerry Abram, who helped me understand better the five-thousand-year-old tradition of Ayurvedic healing which began in India. The course helped me understand what the weird things they were doing to me at the spa were and why. Kerry's words underscored Lisa's message. Kerry explained that about half of people over half of people over age fifty in the western world have chronic conditions that Western medicine doesn't handle very well, but very few of those people take the time to learn about alternate methods of healing, so she commended us for taking the course and venturing into the unknown

Lisa's and Kerry's words also reminded me of the story in the Talmud about the two paths – the short route which is long, and the long route which is short. While I initially thought of these paths as related to Western and Eastern medicine respectively, perhaps they can be understood more broadly as referring to the path of healing and the path of inaction. The route of inaction seems like the shorter route since it requires less effort, but ends up long, because that route is continued pain and suffering. By contrast, the route of healing is the longer route since it requires so much work and so many wrong turns along the way. But ultimately, this path of healing may be shorter, as it can lead out of pain and suffering.

"Healing is costly, but it is an investment in yourself," Lisa said. She also told me to repeat in my head, "I love me, and the universe is providing me everything I need to be happy." I've been repeating these words in my head before bed ever since.

As Lisa massaged each muscle area, she said that I needed to breathe into that area to send oxygen to that region. She said that what I was doing by breathing into the muscles was more important than what she was doing by massaging them. She shared that the director said that with each inhale I should picture that I am breathing in golden sunlight which is spreading to each part of my body. When I exhale, I should picture that the golden light is removing everything from my body everything that I don't need – all toxins and pain. As Lisa massaged me, I imagined that I was lounging by the pool at my grandparents of blessed memory condo in Florida, breathing in the sunlight.

As Lisa massaged each area, she instructed me to think about the muscles she's touching and all they enable me to do. When she massages my legs, I need to think about how my legs allow me to walk and swim and dance. She told me that she touches them, I need to thank them for all they do for me and tell them that I am breathing and sending them more oxygen and love, so that they don't have to work so hard, and they can take a break and relax. Lisa said to tell my muscle: "I'm going to take care of you. I've got you."

Ilana Grinblat

I asked her about her background and how she came to this profession. I imagined that she must have been working in this field for many years to reach this level of expertise. However, to my surprise, she explained that she has only been a massage therapist for a few years. She shared honestly about her problems with alcohol and drug abuse and how these struggles had helped her be able to connect with people's pain and bring healing. She explained:

> *There's a black crystal that when light shines on it, reflects beautiful colors. I see myself as like that crystal. She knows the dark side of life intimately, but as a result, I can bring light and color.*

This idea reminded me of the holiday of *Simchat Torah* this past year which the Open Temple community celebrated by dancing with the Torah on the pier in Venice. Under the lights on the pier, we could see our shadows. "Dance with your shadow." Rabbi Lori had said. "Embrace the dark side of you and dance with it."

Most of my life, I've been a goodie two shoes, but for some reason, this illness had brought out my dark side and forced me to wrestle with (and lose to) my demons. While I think of this as a negative thing, perhaps instead I could think of myself like Lisa does as like the black crystal that can reflect color only because of both the darkness and the light. Rather than trying to make my shadow go away – which it won't –, maybe I could dance with it instead.

This idea is embedded in a tale about the creation of humanity. Jewish tradition teaches that we are each born with two desires – the *yetzer hatov* – our good inclination – and our *yetzer hara* – our evil inclination. The book of Genesis recounts that when God created each part of the natural world, God looked and said that "it was good," but only once God created humanity did God say that it was "very good."

In a *midrash* (interpretation) on Genesis a rabbi named Nahman said in the name a rabbi named Samuel that the saying "it was good" refers to the good desire and the saying "it was very good" refers to our evil desire – because only after creating humanity with both good and bad desires did God say that "it was very good." The text continues:

> *How can the evil desire be very good? That's surprising?!*
>
> *But without the evil desire, however, no man would build a house, take a wife, and beget children*[84]

The rabbi then quotes a verse from Ecclesiastes that says that at the root of all labor and excelling in work is a person's rivalry with their neighbor. (Ecclesiastes 4:4) This text demonstrates the idea that in Jewish tradition, even our bad desires are considered good as they can be channeled to positive purposes.

A legend in the Talmud echoes this idea. In this story, a rabbi named Hanina recounted that once the people fasted prayed for God to capture the evil inclination and give it to them. God did so but told them that if they kill the evil inclination the world will be destroyed (because without a desire to procreate, the world wouldn't continue). So instead of killing the bad inclination, they imprisoned it for three days but as a result, the people searched for a fresh egg throughout the land of Israel and couldn't find one.[85] (Since the urge to reproduce was quashed, the chickens had stopped laying eggs.)

This story underscores the point that our evil inclination can be a good thing. Our passion and striving for more leads us to achieve. Since we can't live without our evil inclination, maybe we can embrace it instead.

Lisa also told me that my glute muscles were underdeveloped and that in order for me to walk, other muscle groups were compensating for the fact that the glute muscles aren't doing their job. "You need to see a physical therapist for glute exercises" she said.

On subsequent days at the spa, different massage therapist worked with me and gave me more insights – offering crucial second and third opinions and more sets of eyes and hands on my body to diagnose and offer solutions. One massage therapist told me that my adductors are

Ilana Grinblat

tight and gave me additional stretches to loosen them. As the African proverb says, "It takes a village," so too, it is taking the collaboration of many gifted, caring healers to repair my body and soul.

That week, when I met with my physical therapist, I relayed to him all the notes that I had asked the massage therapists at the spa to write down. He gave me six new kinds of glute exercises to do each day – which I've added to my daily routine. He also told me that when I'm stressed, I tighten my glute muscles unnecessarily. "If you want to live to enjoy your grandchildren, you need to stop squeezing those muscles." he explained:

> *You're used to putting out three alarm fires all the time, but your body can't handle living like that. You're doing too many things at once. You need to do things one a time. You need to finish one thing before you start the next. You need to change the way you're living. Be kind to yourself, relax and let go, stop striving to become all the time and just be.*

Kerry Abram, my congregant who is a wellness instructor, also gave me similar advice in an email she sent me that week. She wrote:

> *Reflecting on our conversation, given my expertise and training, my strongest impression is that you may get more relief by doing less – much less; FAR less – than you are doing now, and try to rest, breathe, sleep, and simply BE in every spare moment.*

Kerry's words echoed Rabbi Abraham Joshua Heschel's description of/in *The Sabbath*.

Heschel wrote:

> *There is a realm of time where the goal is not to have but to be, not to own, but to give, not to control but to share, not to subdue but to be in accord.*

I guess I'll have to find a way to enter that realm in some measure not only on the Sabbath but each day. One of my healers told me to find a hobby, a way for my brain to shut off. I pointed out that I have many hobbies such as writing, Zumba, and swimming, but he explained that all those activities serve a purpose. None of them turn off my mind. He prescribed a hobby which serves no purpose and allows my mind to disengage. He told me to go home and take a long bubble bath with a candle and scents to engage all my senses. He also said:

> *Don't feel like a unicorn. What you're going through is not unique. Many people go through similar struggles. This is just* when *this is happening to you. If you love yourself as much as you love your children, then nothing will be able to deter you from your path in life.*

While we were talking, he received a text that a friend of his has cancer. Reflecting on the text, he said, "Tomorrow isn't guaranteed, so enjoy today."

These words really go to me. More than anything, I want to live to enjoy my grandchildren! Yet, his statement about loving myself as much as I loved my children puzzled me. I thought I'm supposed to love my children more than I love myself – sacrificing for them and putting their needs before my own. But then I reflected further and realized that I too am someone's child. So perhaps, I do need to love myself as much as I love my children. Indeed, only if I love myself enough can I live long and be healthy enough to be there for them or anyone else for that matter. I went to the store and bought lavender bubble bath and took a long bath.

The next night, I was preparing to teach at Open Temple. Our brilliant administrative guru, Jayne, had recently left to take a new job, and it was my first event that I was running without her help. I was getting stressed about the set up that needed to be completed within the next half hour, which I had never done before. I noticed that I was squeezing my adductor muscles, and I stopped in my tracks.

When I had spoken to my spiritual director, Ashley, she told me to put my hands on my muscles when I speak to them, so I put my hands on my adductors and told them: "I want to live to enjoy my grandchildren, so you don't need to work so hard." I took a deep breath and sent them some extra oxygen and love and told them they could take a break. Then after a moment, I returned to the work I had to do and did it as calmly as I could.

In Kerry's class, she said, "The way you do anything is the way you do everything." For years, I've inadvertently done everything with muscles clenched and tense. Now I need to do everything calmly instead.

After the week was over, I met with the director of the spa for the follow up consultation and she gave me oils, herbs, and advised me to see someone named Mike.

"What does Mike do?" I asked her.

"Mike is Magic," she said.

I haven't yet met Magic Mike – though I did enjoy the movie series by that title! Yet, indeed, when I look back on my week at the spa, the word that comes to mind most is magic – the magic of the loving generosity of Lori to give me this gift, and the caring touch and wise words of Lisa, the director of the spa, Kerry, Ashley, and the other gifted massage therapists – the magic of thousands of years of Ayurvedic healing wisdom, the magic of East and West coming together, the magic of the dark crystal that with light reflects color – the magic of the long, winding route and bravely marching forward toward healing – and dancing with our shadow along the way.

The Prescription

July 30, 2023

At the end of my week at the spa, the director had recommended that I go to see someone named Michael. When I asked what he does, she said only "he's magic." So, I went to see him.

The director was right. Michael is magic. He does Chinese massage therapy which includes massage, cupping, and a few minutes of chanting in Chinese at the end with a necklace of big wooden beads around his arm. I don't know how to describe what he did, but it worked. Within a few weeks of seeing him once a week, my pain was greatly diminished.

At the end of each session, I asked him (as I ask all my healers) for recommendations of what to do until I see him again. I expected him to give me stretches, or a suggestion for a vitamin or a device or type of treatment, as my healers typically do. These prescriptions have been crucial to my recovery over the last year. Michael didn't offer any of those types of medical prescriptions. Instead, what he said surprised me.

"You need to laugh more," Michael said. He recommended I watch comedies as well as "Forever My Girl" on Netflix.

"That's medicine," he said.

I wouldn't normally think of watching movies as medical treatment, but Michael's comment broadened my idea of what I should consider part of my healing regimen.

"You've been looking in the rearview mirror too much," he added. "Instead of looking backward, you need to look forward. You need to plan for what you're going to do, people you're going to see."

These dual recommendations of laughing and looking forward seemed particularly poignant to me and reminded me of the biblical story of Isaac. The first Jewish child recounted in the Torah is named: *Yitzchak* which means: "He will laugh" – the verb for laughter in the future tense. When Sarah, his mother, (who was ninety years old and had stopped menstruating) overheard a messenger say that she was going to have a son, she laughed. When she had a son as the messenger had predicted, she said, "God has brought me laughter; everyone who hears will laugh with me.'"[86]

Sarah spoke of collective laughter in the future tense. She was looking ahead with hope and joy.

Illness has a way of making you look backward. You try to examine the cause of the illness and what could have been done to prevent it. And yet if we get stuck looking backward, we can become overwhelmed with sadness. Like Lot's wife, when we turn back and look at the loss and destruction, we can turn into a pillar of salty tears. But if we look ahead and plan fun activities for the future, perhaps we can turn our frown upside down.

As soon as I left Michael's office, I watched *Forever My Girl* at home. I also asked Jeremy to go to see *My Big Fat Greek Wedding 3* with me in the theaters. In the coming weeks, I made sure to watch YouTube clips of my favorite comedians Trevor Noah, Dulce Sloan, and Roy Wood Jr. frequently.

The last nearly two years of illness have been horrifying, and very serious, so humor is an important corrective. Perhaps as much or even more than stretches and vitamin supplements, laughter is good medicine indeed.

Relinquishing

August 2, 2023

"You can clean out the garage," I told Tal on the phone from the airport when I landed in New Mexico.

"I've been waiting for ten years for you to say that," he replied.

Our garage was filled with many things, but mostly with items for babies and young children – car-seats, clothes, bikes of all sizes, and more. I wanted another child for many years. I didn't want to clean out the garage because as long as we kept those items, I felt like I had the option of having another child. The messiness of the garage never concerned me, but it bothered Tal every time he walked into it.

Although I longed for another child and love that idea, I was too terrified to conceive another child. After three pregnancies, the third of which ended in miscarriage, two labors (the first of which was forty-six hours long with life-threatening complications), I couldn't bring myself to conceive again.

Then my illness took away this option from me. At first, I was too sick to even physically be able to have sex or conceive and then after many months, I was/am still too sick for it to be wise to conceive. Through the last twelve years since my miscarriage, I couldn't go through with conceiving – and I also couldn't give up on the idea. Internally, I debated the idea constantly to no avail.

Apparently, I wasn't alone. There's a saying in the Talmud for when the rabbis argue about a matter endlessly and can't get to a conclusion. The saying is *Teyku* (which means a tie). Even today, when in Israel two teams tie a game, it's called *Teyku*. This word is a Hebrew an acronym for 'The Tishbite will solve the difficulties and problems." The prophet Elijah who is supposed to be the harbinger of redemption in the future was from the village of Tishbe and therefore called the Tishbite. The idea of this acronym is that in the world to come or in a messianic future, Elijah will be able to resolve all lingering legal dispute, but in the meantime, we can't seem to figure it out.

When it came to the idea of a fourth pregnancy, I was *Teyku*. I would debate endlessly within but never could reach a conclusion– until that moment on the phone.

The facts on the ground had changed. I was fifty years old and had been sick for twenty months. So, I finally said the words he'd been waiting to hear for years. I didn't need Elijah to tell me, the dispute was settled. Game over. I do have the two sweetest kids to ever walk this planet (in my unbiased opinion), so I could let the idea of another child go. The time had come. The angel of truth had beat me into submission and it was time for me to admit defeat – to grow up, face painful truths, and relinquish unrealistic fantasies.

The idea of giving up is echoed in a teaching about returning lost objects in Deuteronomy. Moses explained that if a person sees a fellow Israelite's ox or sheep go astray, they must return it to the owner (unless they don't know who the owner is or the owner doesn't live nearby).[87] Like these animals, other lost objects also must be returned to their owners.[88]

The Talmud further explored the extent and limits on this obligation in abundant detail. Twenty-three years ago, in my last year of rabbinical school, my chavruta (friend/study partner) now Rabbi Rachel Rudis (now Bovitz) studied for the tractate of the Talmud called Bava Metzia which deals with the laws of lost objects. For our Talmud exam, we studied the intricacies of the rules that the rabbis (of the third through sixth centuries C.E.) created about how and when a lost item is returned to its owner.

Most of the tractate is extremely tedious – as it explores every possible contingency. For example, the rabbis debate: If a lost object is dropped in a public place and has no identifying markers with which

What Pain Teaches Us

to tell who it belongs to, does the finder get to keep the item or do they need to try to return it to the owner? For how long is the object considered to belong to the owner before it becomes fair game for the finder to keep it?

In this tractate, the rabbis introduce a concept called *yeush* (relinquishment) which means when the person who lost an object is determined to have given up hope of finding it. The idea is that the owner's *yeush* (giving up hope of finding the object) releases the object into the public domain, which means that the find can keep the object. (As the saying goes, "Finders keepers; losers weepers.")

There are two types of *yeush* – *yeush mida'at* (relinquishment with knowledge) and *yeush shelo mida'at* (unwitting relinquishment). *Yeush mida'at* (knowingly relinquishing) happens when the owner either gives up hope of finding the object or when the circumstances are such that a reasonable person would have given up hope of finding it – such as if it's lost in a public place with no characteristics with which to identify it, like a dollar bill dropped on the street.

But *yeush* can happen even without the owner knowing about it. *Yeush shelo mida'at* happens when the owner of the lost object doesn't know that the object is lost but would have given up hope of finding it if they knew that had lost it – like in the case of the money falling on the public street. (I won't bore you with any more of the intricate details!)

I honestly haven't thought much about this tractate in the twenty-two years since we both completed our Talmud exam, and therefore were able to finish rabbinical school. But when giving permission to clean out the garage, I recognized it as a moment of *yeush mida'at* (knowing relinquishment), not of an object, but of a dream. Once I let go of the fantasy, then I could release the items in the garage – and let him take them to Goodwill, so other babies can enjoy them.

At some point during my illness, I had done *yeush shelo mida'at* – unwittingly let go of the dream of another child, but *yeush shelo mida'at* –silent, internal acknowledgment wasn't enough. I had to say the words aloud to let it go – to allow for the cleaning out of what we no longer had use for. Now instead of planning for more kids, I need to

Ilana Grinblat

heal to get well enough to enjoy my children (and with God's help) someday my grandchildren.

Just before the holiday of Passover, there is a ritual which expresses *yeush* (relinquishment). In preparation for Passover, Jews are supposed to remove all leavened bread and other leavened food from their houses in remembrance of the Exodus from Egypt. When the ancient Israelites fled slavery in Egypt, they left in a hurry and didn't have time for their bread to rise, so Jews ever since throughout the world refrain from eating leavened bread and foods on Passover.

Each year, after cleaning the house of every crumb of bread, there is a special ritual which is conducted called *Bedikat Chametz* (checking for leaven). The night before Passover, ten pieces of bread are placed throughout the house. The lights in the home are turned off, and the kids (or adults if there are no kids in the home) look for those pieces of bread using a candle and a feather to sweep the bread into a bag. The bread is then burned, and a special formula is recited which states (in Aramaic).

> *All chametz (leavened product) in my possession which I have not seen or removed, or of which I am unaware, is hereby nullified and ownerless as the dust of the earth.*

I've always loved this ritual (except for the one time when I lit my hair on fire as a kid when I leaned over holding the candle to look for the bread). I love not only the scavenger hunt like quality – but also the idea that you can try your best – clean every speck of bread from your home – but then there comes a time when you must stop and let go. There might be some bread you haven't found or don't know about, but still, the searching must stop at some point – even though you didn't reach perfection.

I always recite this formula after I finish editing each book. I've edited and edited – but surely there will still be errors – but at some point, I have to relinquish them and declare them "nullified and ownerless as the dust of the earth." There's pain in that moment, but also poignancy. You need to stop editing to publish the book, just as you need to stop cleaning to enjoy the holiday.

While the completion Passover cleaning is filled with a fun ritual – with a scavenger hunt, a candle and a feather and a fancy Aramaic formula, some of the most painful, profound moments of *yeush* (letting go) in our lives are short and stark. They might just be one sentence uttered on a cellphone in an airport – like, "you can clean out the garage."

Broken Open Again

August 3, 2023

"You're returning staff from last year." The lady said at check-in at Philmont Scout Camp in New Mexico. "I have your pronouns as she and her. Is that still the case?"

"Yes," I replied.

It was a year exactly from the date that I had checked-in to serve as a chaplain at the camp for the first time. Returning to this place brought a flood of memories back of what my life was like when I was here precisely a year earlier.

While the place looked the same, I felt how much has changed for me in the year. During the year since I had been here, I had left my job and gotten several new jobs, learned how to do those new jobs, stopped being afraid of Covid, published my third book, and written eighty pages of this book. If you had told me a year ago that *any* of these things would happen, I wouldn't have believed you.

Other than my gender pronouns, one thing that has stayed the same in my life is that I'm still sick – unfortunately. I am somewhat healthier than I was a year ago. Last year, I was doing a daily breathing treatment with a breathing machine as I was only a few months after being hospitalized for Covid, and my pelvic pain was more intense and encompassed more surface area in my body than it does now. But sadly, I still get light-headed and had trouble walking between the buildings at the camp today, and the pain is still with me at all times. A year ago, I was on medical leave from my job at the Board of Rabbis and now I am on medical leave from my job at Open Temple since I collapsed at work earlier this summer.

When I came to the bed in the room where the Jewish chaplains stay, I remembered how a year ago, a rabbi named Amy Bernstein, who was Past-President of the Board of Rabbis where I worked had told me I had to stop working while on medical leave. "Let things fall apart," she had told me. "It will be educational for us to know what you do and where we need to step up. Your health is more important."

Thinking back on that conversation, I realize how I didn't follow her advice. I meant to, but I didn't. Now a year later, both Kerry and another one of my healers within the past week have given me different versions of the same instructions. Today, one of the first things I did when getting here was return a call from the job that I'm on unpaid medical leave from to answer a work-related question. The more things change the more they stay the same.

They say that hindsight is 20-20, but my vision is entirely blurred. I don't know if any of the decisions are the right ones. While all those things have changed externally, internally I feel that I've lost my mind, my way, and my moral compass. I can't undo the past year, but I often wish I could. A year ago, the pain was stronger, but my life was simpler, less brutal and sad.

Last year, I was in pain, but this year, I'm in pain and broken-hearted.

Last Friday in Idyllwild, I read from the Torah the passage that is Judaism's most important prayer, the *Shema*, which means to listen and to do what is requested. That passage states, "Therefore put these, My words, on your heart."[89]

The rabbis asked about this verse: Why does God say to put these words "on your heart," rather than "in your heart?"

Rabbi Menachem Mendel of Kotzsk, a rabbi from eighteenth and nineteenth century Poland answered that:

> *Much of the time, a person's heart is closed, not ready to receive these words. Let the words remain outside, on the heart, until the day when circumstances break the heart open, and the words of the Torah can enter.*[90]

I can only hope that now that my heart is broken, that Amy and Kerry's advice will slip into my heart. I hope that this time, I'll not only listen but also follow their words – that I'll change the way that I live – now just where I live but *how* I live – how I do anything and how I do everything.

A year ago, if you had told me I would be this sick a year later, I would have been deeply disappointed to hear that. Where will I be a year from now? I've always assumed that this condition was temporary and that it would end soon. Now, I wonder if that's true.

Is this temporary and time-limited and in a year, will I feel like a million bucks? Or is it a chronic condition aggravated by and perpetuated by stress that I'll have to grapple with for years to come? If so, do I have the power to change it, to heal myself by changing the way I live?

I'll have to dedicate this next year finding out the answers to those questions.

I recently read a powerful book by Dr. Lissa Rankin called, *Mind over Medicine: Scientific Proof that You Can Heal Yourself*. In this book, she recounts how she healed herself from multiple medical conditions by making radical life changes – quitting her job, putting her career on hold for several years and moving with her husband and daughter from the city to a rural nature-filled area.

Looking back on her journey, she explained:

> *My doctors were shocked. With little help from them, I had cured myself from conditions that all conventional medical treatments had previously failed to treat. One doctor told me I had added thirty years to my life. (One told me I looked ten years younger. I didn't believe her until I got carded that night when I ordered a glass of wine.)*

Ilana Grinblat

> *How did I heal myself? Although I also made changes in my diet and exercise regimen, I primarily credit the healing of my mind. I believe yours has the power to heal you too.*
>
> *Although my story may sound suspicious to you, I want you to understand that this s not woo woo metaphysics I'm talking about here. It's simple biochemistry. In my estimation, most of my health conditions were stress-related so making life changes that alleviated the havoc of repetitive stress responses and replaced stress responses with relaxation responses altered the physiology of my body.*[91]

Perhaps if a doctor can heal herself, a rabbi can too!

For the first nineteen months of pain, I was reluctant to make major life changes – waiting until I got better first before making big decisions since my judgement could be clouded by my illness. I was reluctant to put myself through the additional stresses of big changes.

And yet, Dr. Rankin's story suggests that it might be the other way around. Perhaps, only by making radical changes both in my external situation (like where I work) and my internal circumstances (such as how I live) can I get to healing.

If I come back here, a year from now, I wonder where I'll be. How will I look back on where I am now? Will I be in pain, or will I be cured? Will I look back on the decisions I'm making now with crushing regret or with overflowing gratitude? I have no idea.

I can only hope that a year from now, I will have not just listened to my healers and friends but followed their advice. I can only hope that the Torah, the sacred words that my healers, friends, and beloveds have taught me, will have seeped into my broken heart and healed it.

Stubborn Revisited

August 10, 2023

My daughter is hiking up the Tooth of Time today, and I'm not with her.

I remember a year ago how desperately I had wanted to go on that hike. Even though I was in much worse shape physically than I am right now, I was determined to hike to the top of the mountain, and I was so glad that I accomplished that feat.

Now, a year later I have chosen not to go with Hannah today. I could have asked for the day off to join her, but I'm tired. After twenty-one months of pain, I'm really, really, tired.

Over the past ten days that I've been at Philmont, I've felt my body relax. My pain level has been going down. My energy level has been going up, and I don't want to push myself too hard and lose the progress I've made.

I am reminded of the Book of Genesis which recounts that when God created the world,

> *God had finished on the seventh day, God's work which God had made, and God rested on the seventh day from all God's work which God had done, and God blessed the seventh day and declared it holy—having rested on it from all the work of creation that God had done.*[92]

Ilana Grinblat

The rabbis asked a good question on this verse. God doesn't get tired, so why did God need to rest? They answered that God rested to model for people who do get tired the importance of rest.[93]

Last year, I stubbornly climbed the Tooth of Time to nine-thousand feet. This year, I am choosing to follow God's example and rest instead.

At Philmont, each morning, I attend a meeting, and each night I lead a service for people on a field as deer and bunnies walk by. For the rest of the day, I'm on call if anyone needs to speak to a chaplain or needs transportation, but so far, no one has called. Hannah is in activities which are open to the family of staff, and I am having some quiet time. I do my stretches and write and am discovering the healing power of being alone.

Also in Genesis, after creating the first person, Adam, God said:

"It is not good for humanity to be alone,"[94] and so God created Eve as a helping partner for Adam.

This verse has been so important to me in my illness – reminding me to call on others to help me as needed. And yet, now, after twenty months of being dependent on others (and sometimes not well enough to be left alone), I'm finding that it is good to be alone sometimes. Right now, quiet, solitary time, feels like the best medicine for my body and soul. When I have my own space, the muscles in my body let go and unwind.

The joy that I'm finding in solitude is especially strong nowadays when I am alone in nature. At Philmont, New Mexico, I enjoy watching exquisite sunrises and sunsets against the backdrop of tree covered mountains, puffy clouds, and brightly colored skies and star-filled skies at night. I love watching families of bears, deer, raccoons and even turkeys. This state truly lives up to its slogan as "God's country." What Kerry said about Idyllwild is also true of rural New Mexico: "here, God is a local call."

Yesterday, one of my fellow chaplains at Philmont, a Christian pastor, chose to offer a prayer by Rabbi Nachman of Breslov (of eighteenth/nineteenth century Ukraine.

What Pain Teaches Us

Master of the universe, grant me the ability to be alone.
May it be my custom to go outdoors each day,
Among the trees and grass, among all growing things,
And there may I be alone, and enter into prayer
To talk with the One to whom I belong.

May I express there everything in my heart,
And may all the foliage of the field –
All grasses, trees, and plants – awake at my coming,
To send the powers of their life into the words of my prayer
So that my prayer and speech are made whole
Through the life and spirit of all growing things,
Which are made as one by their transcendent source.

May I then pour out the words of my heart
Before Your Presences like water, God,
And lift up my hands to You in worship
On my behalf, and that of my children.

This prayer reminds me of a story about a boy who went out to the woods every afternoon. His family was deeply worried since he snuck off every day for hours and they never knew when he would return.

One day, his father confronted him and asked him:

Ilana Grinblat

> *"Why do you go out into the forest every day?"*
>
> *"I go to be with God,"* the boy answered.
>
> The father replied, *"Don't you know that God is the same everywhere?"*
>
> The boy replied, *"I know, but I'm not."*[95]

Indeed, my time at Philmont this year has reminded me that I too am not the same everywhere. Here I feel more myself than I've felt in a long time. As I return to Los Angeles, sadly and reluctantly, I hope that I can follow the example of that boy and of Rabbi Nachman of Breslov's to find solace in the blessings of solitude in nature daily – or at least as often as I can.

As stubborn as I was to climb the mountain, I'll need to be just as stubborn about my need for rest, quiet, and nature.

Just Rest

August 29, 2023

As soon as I got in my car, I started to cry.

I had held in the tears all day since my doctor's appointment. I'd contained my emotions through the tutoring of the bar mitzvah student, and the open house for prospective students, through the meetings with my colleagues, and the phone calls with my children. But as soon as I got in the car, I knew my workday was over, and the tears began to fall

My doctor's appointment hadn't gone well.

On Saturday night, while at my in-laws for dinner, I stopped being able to walk or even hold my head up at the table. Since it was late at night, urgent care was closed, so I went to sleep and went to urgent care the next morning. At urgent care, they gave me intravenous fluids and took my blood for testing. I then went to the doctor the next day to get the results of the blood tests.

At the appointment, my primary care physician told me that one test called ANA was positive – and not just a little positive but very positive. This test is a marker for autoimmune issues. Based on this test, she explained that she thought I had an autoimmune disease but didn't know which one, and I needed to see a rheumatologist.

I called the rheumatologist my doctor referred me to and the soonest appointment they had was a month away.

So again, I was back to square one – back to the hardest part – when they know something's wrong with me, but they don't know what. Or maybe I had never left that part.

It's now been twenty-one and half months since the polyp removal, and still not healthy. Overall, the pain is going down, but my energy level is decreasing too. My strength comes and goes. I get lightheaded just from standing up, and my ability to walk comes and goes.

"Since the pain was going down, I had thought I was in the home stretch of this nightmare," I told one of my healers, "but apparently not." "I want to stay." I told him, "As painful as it is, I want to stay (alive)."

"We're all on our way somewhere," he said, but "don't put dirt on yourself just yet," he said.

"But that's what I do for a living," I said. "I write eulogies."

"Don't write this one just yet." He replied and explained:

"This whole time, we couldn't figure out why you weren't getting better. Maybe this is the beginning of finding an answer. Having something to fight against is better than not knowing what you're fighting against. Maybe they can put you on a special diet so you can manage your life better."

"I don't want to have an autoimmune disease. I want to be healthy," I said.

"And I want to be eighteen again," he said.

He then told me, "You might have to slow down. Maybe instead of doing all your stretches, you could do just some of them – the ones that you feel are most beneficial. I know you want to put the pedal to the metal, but you can't do it all at once."

"But I like all my stretches," I objected.

"Maybe you can't do all of them in one day. You could split them up and do half of them on one day and the other half the next day." He even told me that maybe I should stop swimming for a while. Maybe it was too hard on my body right now. I objected, saying that the daily swimming is why my EKG is good, why my heart is strong. My mother had died at age 62 of heart disease and for that reason, I exercise daily to keep my heart strong. My healer had told me to start swimming daily in response to the pelvic pain, but now he was telling me to stop. I was crestfallen.

This conversation made two teachings in the Torah portion of that week resonate for me in a new way. In the Torah portion called *Ki Tavo* which means when you come, the people approached the Promised Land after nearly forty years of wandering in the desert. As they near the land, Moses detailed to them the wonderful blessings that would occur if they follow God's instructions when they get there and the curses that would befall them if they don't.

One of the curses is:

> *In the morning you will say, "If only it were evening," and in the evening you shall say, "if only it were morning," because of what your heart shall dread, and your eyes shall see.*[96]

Commenting on this verse, Rabbi Harold Kushner of blessed memory wrote:

> *Bad as the reality will be, you will fear that the future will be worse. Fear of misfortune is often worse than the actual misfortune as our imaginations conjure up all sorts of dreadful experiences we may feel we deserve.*[97]

Tell me about it!

As soon as I heard that I might have an autoimmune disorder, my mind raced to the worst possible outcomes – a life of paralysis and dependence on others, and death. This idea is called catastrophizing – or as my healer said, "putting dirt on myself." I was ready to bury myself before even finding out the prognosis. The best possible outcome was something far better – perhaps something treatable with

Ilana Grinblat

a medicine or a special diet – a way to regain my strength and find my way out of this illness. While I assumed the worst, it was also possible that there was a path forward to healing instead.

By contrast to the long list of bone-chilling curses, Moses also described beautiful blessings that would come to the people if they behaved well. Moses said,

> *All these blessings shall come to you and reach you, if you listen to the voice of God, your God.*[98]

On this verse, Rabbi Kushner wrote:

> *Sometimes God intends to bless us, but we are so busy running after success that the blessings cannot catch up to us. Instead of chasing after fulfillment perhaps we need to slow down and let the good things in life catch up to us.*[99]

This idea is echoed in the Talmud, which states:

> *From one who runs after greatness, greatness flees. But one who runs away from greatness, greatness follows. One who forces time is forced back by time. One who yields to time finds time standing by their side.*[100]

Perhaps this saying could apply to health as well. For twenty-one months, I had been running after health, and it has fled from me. Maybe now, I would have to slow down, so health can catch up with me.

I had planned to teach these verses and commentaries at Torah study on Friday. On Friday morning, I woke up at 5 am, went to the gym and did my swimming and stretches (despite my healer's advice) and then when I got to work, I lost my ability to walk, talk, and hold my head up. My dad had to come to take me to the urgent care – for the second time this week. There, I was given IV fluids again, but I still felt and looked terrible, and they sent me to the emergency room and later admitted me to the hospital where I have been for two days so far as they run blood tests, an MRI and a CT scan to try to figure out why I keep losing my strength.

I must slow down after all – since now I am just lying in my hospital bed all day – and it looks like I'll have to go on medical leave from my job again – after only two weeks back at work – my third medical leave of this year. Oy!

In the emergency room, I felt like I was back to square one. Here, Tal and I were again in the same hospital we had been twenty-one months ago with me in pain, unable to sit up and the doctors not knowing what's wrong with me. Again, the doctors were reluctant to admit me to the hospital and were trying to send me home with some painkillers and no answers as to the cause of the problem. Again, I felt like my pain wasn't being heard and taken seriously enough.

But this time, we were wiser. We didn't let them send me home with some pills and no answers. Tal, my dad, and I advocated strongly and convinced them to admit me to the hospital, to run the tests which we hoped would figure why I was still so sick, twenty-one months into this medical nightmare.

Tal, my father and my stepmother took shifts sitting with me, advocating for/with me, and bringing me food and books. Lori and I spoke on the phone, and she encouraged me not to worry about the congregation. She had it all under control. One of my healers texted me: "Just Rest!"

I can't write the conclusion to this chapter, to this journey just yet. From my hospital bed, as I wait to be taken to the MRI and the CT scan, I have no answers. But like it or not, I am slowing down, and letting the blessing -- the love of my family and friends catch up with me. I hope that health will soon follow and catch up with me too.

Relief

September 11, 2023

I feel elated. I don't have a rheumatological disease.

Or to be more precise, the rheumatologist feels confident that I don't have a rheumatological disease. She wants to take further bloodwork to be sure and see me back in two weeks but based on her exam, she feels fairly certain that I don't have an autoimmune disease.

So, the last few weeks of worrying were a false alarm. My primary care physician had told me that my ANA levels were high – very high – and this meant that I had an auto-immune disease, but I would have to see the rheumatologist in order to ascertain which disease I had.

The soonest rheumatologist appointment I could get was a month away, so I called each day to see whether there was a cancellation, and I was able to move the appointment up by a few days, but not by much.

The night before the appointment, I had trouble sleeping. This prospect was overwhelming. I didn't know what to root for. No auto-immune disease sounded good. Any autoimmune disease sounded like something I would have to deal with for the rest of my life, not for a finite time period, so I was terrified.

At the appointment, the rheumatologist asked me a long list of horrifying questions of possible awful scenarios, such as:

Do you have rashes on your body that don't go away for months at a time?

Ilana Grinblat

Do you have pains in your joints that feel like someone is stabbing you?

The list of questions with terrible-sounding prospects went on and on.

Thankfully, I am not having any of the symptoms on her list, which is why she doesn't think that I have an auto-immune disease.

After this appointment – and this false alarm experience, I have a greater appreciation for a prayer in Judaism that is traditionally said daily. The prayer called *"Asher Yatzar* (Who Created)" which is traditionally recited after defecation. The prayer reads:

> *Blessed are You, Lord our God, Sovereign of the Universe, who created the human being with wisdom and created within the person many openings and cavities. It is obvious and known before Your throne of glory that if one of them opened or became blocked, it would be impossible to sustain ourselves and to stand before you even for an hour. Blessed are You, who heals all flesh and works wonders.*

While I've known this prayer for many years, the prayer now means more to me than ever.

The rheumatologist's long list of questions reminded me just how many things can go wrong with one's body and how extremely fragile each body is. If one thing goes wrong (which can be something as simple as not drinking enough water or having a reaction to a medication), we can be down for the count – as I was the day I ended up in the hospital. At the same time, the prayer reminds me how extraordinarily intricate the workings of the body are and what an incredible miracle the process of healing is.

I say this prayer of gratitude today.

Normal

October 3, 2023

"You're only having aches, not pains, so you can return to your life now," one of my healers said.

"I can't go back to it," I replied. "It's destroyed."

It was nearly twenty-two months from the polyp removal and surely it was a moment I had been waiting for the entire time – a relatively clean bill of health. I am not done healing, but I am headed in the right direction. I received this pronouncement that I was healed enough to return to regular functioning, but it was hardly the joyful moment I had imagined.

I was profoundly grateful that my pain had lessened enough that what remained was an amount I could live with – finally! My energy level and strength were improving slowly but surely. I had increased my swimming from half an hour to an hour a day, and I could now reliably walk without needing to stop along the way. My meal plan from the nutritionist was helping, along with the two liters of water I was now drinking each day. Finally, my pain was going down, and my energy was going up – both vectors headed appreciably in the right direction. Halleluyah!

But my life was in shambles. I felt like I was standing on an island after a hurricane, surveying the damage. The twenty-two months of illness had cost me three jobs. When my illness began, I was working at the Board of Rabbis which I left for medical reasons. I then got a new job at Temple Beth Shalom (which I also had to leave due to the

Ilana Grinblat

pain) and then I got a job at Open Temple, which I again had to go on medical leave from (after I collapsed at work and had to be taken to the hospital twice, a few months apart). Now, it's not clear if they want me back in the same capacity when my leave concludes or in a drastically reduced way. Also, Temple Har Shalom of Idyllwild doesn't have anyone to step forward to become President after Dec 31, so they might close. So, currently I am on leave from my main job, and both my jobs are in jeopardy.

So, once I finish getting my health and my weight back, I will have to fix my job situation and get out of limbo professionally.

My "normal" life isn't there to go back to.

My healer mentioning the world "normal" reminded of previous conversation we had months ago about that word. I had shown him how a part of me wasn't working right. "That's not normal," I told him.

"There is no normal," he replied, and started telling me true stories of various maladies that show that there's a huge range of how the body operates.

That brief interchange had stayed with me – the idea that there's no "normal." So perhaps my "normal" life isn't there to come back to because there's no such thing as a "normal" life to begin with.

Indeed, there is no word for normal in the Bible. The Modern Hebrew word for normal is *normali* –taken from the English because there is no such concept in Hebrew literature. (Modern Hebrew only borrows from English when it lacks an idea entirely in its own lexicon.) So, there are no words for or stories about normalcy in the Bible or in all of Jewish literature.

Yet, there are many stories of healing – many stories of reconstructing after a wreckage – most notably perhaps, that of Noah after the flood that destroyed the world.

I recall a column I wrote for the Jewish Journal in 2016, long before my illness began. The reflection was about the biblical story where after the flood, Noah sent a dove out to survey the damage. The verse reads:

What Pain Teaches Us

> *The dove returned to him in the evening, and behold, it had plucked an olive leaf in its mouth.*[101]

Reflecting on this verse, I wrote:

When the dove returns with the olive leaf, Noah stays in the ark. Seven days later, when the dove flies away forever, Noah still remains in the ark — until God tells him to leave. Then Noah plants a vineyard, drinks the wine and dances naked in his tent. Traumatized by the destruction he witnessed, Noah turns to alcohol for comfort.

As I write these words, many people whose homes were devastated by Hurricane Florence in the Carolinas are awaiting word whether it is safe for them to return home. The hard work of rebuilding their lives has not yet begun. A year after Hurricane Maria in Puerto Rico, there are still families without homes or a roof over their heads, and the lightless streets are impassable at night. Noah's story reminds us that the work of reconstruction after a flood or other calamity can extend long after the stories leave the headlines.

Likewise, healing from other traumas often begins significantly after the event itself — after we feel physically safe enough to grapple with the emotional pain. Grief can strike long after a death, and we may not even recognize initially that the sadness we're feeling is a response to that loss, rather than to current events in our lives. Community members typically help at the time of a death but may forget that the hardest time for mourners often comes months or years later.

After the waters recede, the slow, painstaking work of healing begins.

I guess now, the same is true for me. The waters of my illness are receding – thank God – and thanks to my amazing healers' caring dedication. Now, the long, painful project of rebuilding begins for me.

It won't be the work of going back to my life as before. Instead, it'll be moving forward, to build a different future. This new life will be far from perfect and far from normal. Still, I hope it will contain joy, love, and truth.

War

October 7, 2023

At 4:30 AM in the morning on October 7th, my phone starting pinging with text messages. Israel was at war. That night was supposed to be the happiest holiday of the year. We were to be dancing with the Torah on the beach for the holiday of Simchat Torah (which means the Joy of Torah). Instead, Hamas had staged an attack on Israel, unlike any that Israel had ever known.

The information came in bits and pieces, but when the dust settled, it became clear that day was the deadliest day in Jewish history since the Holocaust – with more than 1200 Jews murdered, many thousands wounded, and over 200 Jews taken hostage by Hamas. Young adults at a music festival were raped and murdered, whole families were slaughtered in their homes, and babies were beheaded.

That night, at Simchat Torah, we recited the prayer for the captives, the prayer for the Israeli soldiers, and the prayer for the injured. While leading the service and carrying the Torah, I injured my back.

Whereas I had felt that I was close to the end of my health problems, now I was immobilized again. Yet, I was acutely aware of how my pain was nothing compared to the anguish felt by those in Israel and I recognized how fortunate I am to be living in safety.

I remembered years ago, when I had accidentally dropped the kitchen trashcan on my toe and had to have surgery on my toenail. When I was recovering from the procedure, I was watching on television as the mother of an Israeli teenager who had been kidnapped

Ilana Grinblat

spoke on CNN. Across the world, I felt their agony radiating through the television screen. I was in pain and immobilized and yet the anguish that she and her family were enduring was so much worse.

At that time, I thought of how one part of me, my toenail had been injured – and therefore my whole body was unable to stand. I realized that the Jewish people is also like a body. When one of us is harmed, all of us ache.

At that time, I wrote a prayer based on the Asher Yatzar – the blessing for the body (which is in the "relief" chapter), adapted to be a prayer for the Jewish people.

Tzur Chayeinu, asher yatzar et am yisrael v'umot ha'olam b'chochmah, uvarah bahem mishpachot, mischpachot, yeladim, yeladim. Galui v'yadua lifnei kiseh kvodechah she' im nifga echad mehem or yehareg echad mehem, kulanu koavim. Baruch Ata Adonei, rofe amenu, b'nai yisrael, rofe et umot ha-olam u'mafli la'asot.

Rock of Our Lives, You created the people Israel, and the peoples of the world with wisdom, and created in them interconnected families and children. It is clear and known before the throne of Your Glory, that if one Jew or if one innocent person is injured or killed, all of us are pained. Blessed are You, our God, please heal our people, the children of Israel, heal the people of the world, and work Your wonders, and let us say Amen.

I recite that prayer today:

for the Israelis kidnapped by Hamas – may they be returned safely,

for the soldiers defending Israel – may they be protected,

for the innocent civilians – may they be kept safe,

and for the Jewish people around the world who are aching – may we be healed.

The Good Lord

October 20, 2023

I had just found out that one of my jobs was being scaled back due to budgetary reasons, so I was looking for work. I was concerned since I had more expenses now than before – such as my medical bills. I had also hurt my back, so I was seeing one of my healers to see if he could fix it.

I shared my work worries.

"The Good Lord will send you where you are meant to go," he said.

That sounded good, but I wasn't even sure God works that way. As a rabbi, of course, I'm supposed to have faith, but I wasn't sure. With over 200 hostages having been taken by Hamas in Gaza, and over 1200 killed in the past week, God certainly had bigger problems to worry about than my job situation.

But still, I kept mulling over that idea which made me think about it differently. If God was going to send me somewhere to be of service, where would God want me to go? Then instead of being worried, I could simply be facilitating this process of God sending me on my next adventure. Instead of begging for work and feeling insecure, I could instead reach out to colleagues to see what possibilities they might have available. God was sending me, all I needed to do was help nudge the process along.

If only it were so simple.

A few weeks later, I didn't get one of the jobs that I applied for. "Then it's not meant to be," he said. "The best is yet to come."

I was struck by that phrase and the idea that the best is yet to come. I wasn't sure that I believed it. Looking back on my life, the most enjoyable moments have been when my kids were smaller, and I played with them more. I recall fondly building towers with Jenga blocks with Jeremy and Hannah or sitting and rolling a ball back and forth with them. With the kids about to be grown, I essentially feel that the best years of my life are behind me.

But these words challenged me. Perhaps, I was thinking too narrowly, and not giving life enough credit for its ability to surprise me. Even in these two horrible years, there have been unexpected positive blessings.

Indeed, this positive orientation toward time, the idea that the future could be better than the present is essential in Judaism. The Jewish calendar is lunar, following the cycles of the moon. Each Hebrew month begins when the moon is at its smallest sliver so that the moon only gets bigger and brighter from there.

This increase in light is mirrored in the practice of lighting Hanukkah candles. The ancient rabbis debated the best way to light Hanukkah candles. One group following a rabbi named Shammai said that on the first night of Hanukkah, one should light eight candles and then decrease each night by one candle. Another group following a rabbi named Hillel suggested beginning with one candle on the first night and increasing from there. Each side gave arguments to support its opinion. Hillel's group won the debate because of their view that "In matters of holiness, we increase and don't decrease."[102] In other words, Hillel believe that when it comes to holiness, the best is always yet to come.

In a poignant article called "How the Jewish People Invented Hope," Rabbi Jonathan Sacks of blessed memory noted that God's first word in the Torah *"yehi* (let there be)," is in the future tense.[103] Likewise, when Moses asks God for God's name, God answers, *Ehyeh asher Ehyeh* (I will be what I will be). So, both God's first word and the name that God chose to be named are in the future tense.

What Pain Teaches Us

Likewise, the Torah concludes with the Israelites about to enter the land of Israel after forty years of wandering in the desert. As Sacks noted:

> *The Jewish story ends, as Moses' life ended, with a glimpse of the land not yet reached, a future not yet realized."*
>
> *The same is true of Jewish belief Judaism is the only civilization whose golden age is in the future: the messianic age, the age of peace when "nation will not lift up sword against nation"…This ultimately was the dividing line between Judaism and Christianity. To be a Jew is to reply to the question "Has the messiah come?" with the words "Not yet.* [104]

Sacks further explained:

> *Human beings are the only life form capable of using the future tense. Only beings who can imagine the world other than it is are capable of freedom. And if we are free, the future is open, dependent on us. We can know the beginning of our story but not the end…Judaism, the religion of freedom, is faith in the future tense.* [105]

When I look ahead at my life, I feel tremendous fear and uncertainty about where to go from here. Yet, I am reminded to hold onto faith in the future tense. The story of the rest of my life is unwritten. The best might just be yet to come.

Lost and Found

October 24, 2023-November 30, 2023

Shortly after the October 7th massacre by Hamas on Israel, I received an email from someone I hadn't heard from in thirty years. He had reached out to tell me how sorry he was to hear about the violence in Israel and see the hatred playing out toward Jews around the world. He is Greek Orthodox Christian, but he wanted me to know that he supports Israel and the Jewish people.

His name is Kostadis. He had been my boyfriend in college for three years until the weekend before college graduation, when our relationship had ended badly, and we hadn't spoken since.

The email exchange became a series of phone calls. We talked through unfinished business about how and why our relationship ended. We apologized and cried a lot about the regrets we both still carried. Apparently, time doesn't heal old wounds – only forgiveness does.

Then I told him about the last nearly two years of my life – about the illness and all it left in its wake. I told him of all I had lost in these two years.

"But you found yourself," he said.

His words echoed the ancient ones in Genesis:

*"Lech lecha. (*Go to/for yourself)"

Those words that God told Abram, the ones that started the journey that became the Jewish people, rang in my ears.

Ilana Grinblat

I hadn't thought of it that way, but I guess Kostadis is right.

Over the last two years, with all that I have lost, I did find my will to live. I found my will to do whatever it took to stay alive and get out of pain. I found a part of myself that longs for joy, even if I don't know yet know the path to find it. I found a part of myself that wants to be honest about all that is broken.

I found friends and family who show me that they love me, even when I fall apart, even when I screw up royally, who are willing to accept me with all my flaws, who will walk with me through all the heartbreaks, and who want me to be happy.

On Friday night, I lead services for Temple Har Shalom by zoom and as usual, I came to the *misheberach*, the prayer for those who are ill. For this prayer, I read a list of names gathered by the congregational president of those who are ill and then I ask the congregants to add the names of whoever they would like to add. It was November 17th, 2023, a month shy of two years since the polyp removal procedure. For the first time since the polyp removal procedure, I said the blessing for healing without including my own name as one of the sick people in need of prayers.

I still need to get stronger, but I am not in real pain and no longer sick. That prayer wasn't a real celebration. It was just a quiet moment that perhaps no one noticed but me, but was profound nonetheless.

In all this time, I think I envisioned the end of this being more dramatic, more joyful even. As I come out of pain, I still feel intense sadness. I am wrestling with my own uncertainty, with the wreckage that the storm of the illness left in its wake. I don't know how to move forward from here personally or professionally. My health is still fragile and inconsistent. I am weary in body, mind, and spirit, but moving forward slowly, one step at a time.

This Sunday, November 26, 2023 to mark the second anniversary of Esther's death, I stood at the Esther's gravesite and officiated at the unveiling of the tombstone. I stood together with my friend Deborah and our families and friends.

What Pain Teaches Us

Again, the Torah portion for that day was that of Jacob wrestling by the riverside and again, I shared Esther's poem about the river. I noted how Jacob was injured by wrestling with the angel who wrenched his hip from his socket and changed his name from Jacob (which means crooked) to Israel (which means one who wrestles with God). That night became a turning point for him because previously whenever Jacob had faced a difficult situation, he handled it by cheating, lying, and running away. The encounter with Esau was the first time that he handled a scary situation honestly.

After his encounter with Esau, the Torah recounts that Israel arrived *shalem* (whole) to the city of Shehem. Even though Israel was injured, since he was truthful about it, he was whole.

At the graveside, I said that while we normally think of wholeness and brokenness as opposites, if we're honest about it, we can find wholeness even in our brokenness – if we walk through our pain together.

Deborah spoke beautifully. She said that she never could have gotten through the last two years without the love of her family and friends. She also said:

> *If I've learned anything from the last two years is that we need to accept one another without judging and with compassion. That when we see someone, we shouldn't rush to judge and instead be curious about what they are going through.*

I held my emotions at bay for the beginning of the service, but Deborah's words brought me to tears, and we all wept together.

I shared at the service that we wish that Esther was still with us in body. We wished we were skiing, surfing, swimming, or having dinner with Esther instead of standing at Esther's grave, and no words could change that or take away that pain.

Indeed, if I had a magic wand, I would go back in time and undo the last two years and have Esther still be alive and not have removed the polyp from my cervix. If I could undo it, I would in a heartbeat. Even in hindsight, the sufferings of the last two years are not dear to me.

Yet I can't undo it, so all I can do, like Deborah, is to try to articulate what I've learned. So what did I learn?

I've learned about the power of family, friends, and community to lift us up when we fall. I've learned about the power of healers of both Western and Eastern medicine to be our partners and guides on the winding path of healing. I've learned that the unseen can be even more powerful than the seen. I've learned about the power of truth – that only if we stop running away and lying and honesty face the depth of our struggles do we have a chance of finding wholeness.

I learned that even when life forces us to go on journeys we rather not take, we still might find ourselves along the way. And I learned even when I don't know where I'm going, to get up each morning and just keep trying day by day.

Epilogue

Epilogue

June 25, 2024

"How are you?" A protestant chaplain asked me as I walked towards the Philmont office.

"Good," I said and realized that I meant it, for the first time in a long time.

It has been seven months since Esther's unveiling – two and a half years since my pain began. I am back in Philmont, New Mexico, for the third time in the last two years, serving as a chaplain at the scout camp.

As I return to this place, I am flooded with memories. I see the table in the room where I'm staying, and I remember how two years ago, I put on that table the contraption for my medicine which made it into an inhaler to do my breathing treatments just a month after being in the hospital with Covid. I look at the floor, and I remember doing my stretches there a year ago. As I check in with the medical staff, I remember how low my blood pressure was last year when they took it, and how I got dizzy walking between the buildings. I remember sitting on the bed in the room where I am staying, and Rabbi Amy Bernstein telling me by Zoom to stop working while I was on medical leave from my job at the Federation. I remember a year later, Kerry giving me the same advice while I was on medical leave from Open Temple.

Returning to the same place, I can finally see how far I've come. Unlike two years ago, this year I don't need to take medicine to breathe well. Two years ago, the idea of me hiking up the Tooth of Time sounded absurd to my family. Now, they have no objection. I've hiked this week to see one of the two footprints in the world of a Tyrannosaurs Rex from 65-70 million years ago. Whereas last year, I felt too tired to hike, on yesterday's hike, instead of struggling to keep up, I felt that we were walking too slow!

It feels good to walk around the camp without getting dizzy – to hike without difficulty, to drive on the bumpy dirt roads in the back country without being in pain every time the car jiggles, and to not have to do hours of stretches because of the pain. This year, hiking is no longer an act of stubbornness.

As I return to Philmont, again, I am struck by how much has happened in the past year – so much lost and gained.

I made a list: In the past year, I:

Got out of pain

Regained my physical health and strength

Lost a job

Nearly lost but then retained another job

Regained my friendship with Kostadis

Published my third book

Wrote this book.

What a year of losses and gains!

Now finally, I can see how far I've come. With the help of her angel, Hagar was able to see the well of water that was right in front of her all along. Thanks to my angels – my healers, family, and friends – I am finally out of pain and can see the arc of my healing in its entirety. I can now see the well of love that was there in front of me all along.

What Pain Teaches Us

In many ways, I am still struggling with the aftermath of two years of illness – with lingering sadness and with having lost my main job (due to budgetary issues). But when I look at the list of the past year's losses and gains, I realize how getting OUT of the prison of pain and regaining my health and strength was by far the most difficult and important accomplishment and blessing. As many grandmothers have told me, health is the most important thing because without your health, you have nothing.

If I'm healthy and out of pain, then I can get a job, do enjoyable activities, put my energy into meaningful endeavors and spend time with people who make me happy. But without my health, none of that is possible.

A year ago, while I was bouncing around the jeep in the beautiful back country of New Mexico, I felt happy even though I was in pain. In that moment, I discovered that it was possible for me to be happy and in pain at the same time. But it's hard for me to be happy while in physical pain. When I am out of pain, my chances of happiness improve significantly.

Since I am at this scout camp, the Torah portion for this week couldn't possibly be more perfect since it contains the story of the scouts. After years of wandering in the desert, when the Israelites approached the Promised Land, God told Moses to send twelve scouts to survey the land and report back to the people. The scouts visited the land and reported that it was beautiful, "flowing with milk and honey," the cities were well fortified, and the people were strong. On these facts, all twelve scouts agreed, but they disagreed on what to do. Ten of the scouts believed that they shouldn't go into the land, but Caleb said, "We can surely go up, and we shall gain possession of it, for we can do it." Joshua agreed with this positive outlook.

As a result of the fear inducing report of the ten scouts, the people lost their nerve, and therefore had to stay in the desert until a new generation emerged. Then Joshua and Caleb led this new generation into the land. This story shows the importance of a 'can-do' attitude. To achieve a goal, we need to have faith that it's possible.

Ilana Grinblat

Over the past two years, both the positive outlook of Joshua and Caleb and the fears of the other ten scouts lived within me. I hoped that one day I would get out of the prison of pain, although there were certainly times when I was afraid that I'd never escape. When I lost hope, my healers, friends, and family lifted me up (literally and spiritually) more times than I can count.

The past two years have felt much like wandering in a desert – unsure which path to take. Some of the treatments that I tried helped and some didn't. It was definitely a winding road with lots of wrong turns and dead ends from which I needed to change course. The way into pain was fast; the way out of pain was slow and winding. I'm grateful for all the moments where my healers, friends, and family offered me the voice of Joshua and Caleb, encouraging me that I could persevere. As a result of their kindness and dedicated efforts (along with my own stubbornness), I have thankfully left the prison of pain and emerged into a freer place.

A year ago, I sat on the bed I'm sitting on now and wrote these questions and reflections:

Where will I be a year from now? I've always assumed that this condition was temporary and that it would soon end. Now, I wonder if that's true.

Is this temporary and time-limited and in a year, will I feel like a million bucks? Or is it a chronic condition aggravated by and perpetuated by stress that I'll have to grapple with for years to come? If so, do I have the power to change it, to heal myself by changing the way I live?

I'll have to dedicate this next year to finding out the answers to those questions.

If I come back here, a year from now, I wonder where I'll be. How will I look back on where I am now? Will I be in pain, or will I be cured? Will I look back on the decisions I'm making now with crushing regret or with overflowing gratitude? I have no idea.

Now a year later, I know the answers to these questions. Thanks to God and my angels – my healers, family, friends, and community, and dare I say my own stubborn efforts, I am cured. Thankfully, this wasn't a chronic condition that I will have to grapple with for the rest of my life. I feel tremendous compassion and awe for those who grapple with chronic pain for a lifetime and persevere.

A year ago, as I typed on this computer lying on this bed, I wrote down two hopes: The first was:

I can only hope that a year from now, I will have not just listened to my healers and friends but followed their advice.

Over the past year, due to budgetary concerns, one of my jobs was scaled back, so I had no choice but to follow the advice of my healers and friends to slow down. So that hope came true.

I found that too much time alone without much to do can become its own prison, if I'm not careful to reach out to family, friends, and community when I feel isolated. I am now working on finding ways to serve and meaningful projects to engage my mind and heart.

My second hope was:

I can only hope that the Torah, the sacred words that my healers, friends, and beloveds have taught me, will have seeped into my broken heart and healed it.

While my body has healed, my mind and heart are still on the mend. My mind is unsure of what direction to take going forward. Thankfully, my heart is no longer broken, just battered, bruised, and tender to the touch. I hope that the next year will allow my heart further healing and my mind some more clarity about where to go from here.

In the coming year, I pray that my heart can stay broken open enough for the Torah that my beloved healers, family, and friends

Ilana Grinblat

teach me to get in and work its healing magic. I hope that I can listen to the voices of Joshua and Caleb within and without and bring that can-do attitude to the task of rebuilding my life from the ashes of this illness.

In the meantime, I can now say with a full heart: *Min hametzar karati Yah, anani b'merchav Yah.* From the narrow place, I called out to You, God, and You have answered me with divine, wide-open expanse.[106]

Baruch Ata Adonai Eloheinu Melech Ha'olam Matir Asurim.

Blessed are you God, Sovereign of the Universe, who frees prisoners.

Glossary of Jewish Terms:

Asher Yatzar: Hebrew for who created. This prayer expressed gratitude for the workings of the body. The prayer is traditionally recited after defecation.

Ashrei: Hebrew for "happy are they who." This is the first word of Psalm 145 which is attributed to being composed by King David in the tenth century B.C.E. This psalm is traditionally recited three times daily in Jewish prayer.

Babylonian Talmud: A collection of teachings of rabbis compiled in sixth century Babylonia.

B'nai Mitzvah: Hebrew for children of commandment. This term is the plural of a bar or bat mitzvah – the Jewish coming of age rituals that typically takes place at age thirteen. These ceremonies typically involve the teenager chanting from the Torah, leading prayers, giving a speech about the Torah portion, and doing a community service project. This term is also used for coming-of-age ceremonies for non-binary teenagers who don't identify as either male or female.

B.C.E.: An abbreviation for before the Common Era, also known as B.C.

Bubby: The Yiddish word for grandmother.

C.E.: An abbreviation for the Common Era, also known as A.D.

Challah: Braided bread that is traditionally eaten on the Sabbath.

Chaver: Hebrew for friend. This word is used for a male friend or more generally for a friend without specifying the gender of the friend.

Chaverah: Hebrew for female friend.

Chevruta: From the Hebrew word chaver which means friend. *Chevruta* refers to a study partner for learning Torah and rabbinic texts.

Emet: Hebrew for truth.

Hanukkah: Hebrew for dedication. This holiday also known as the Festival of Lights is a Jewish festival celebrating the recovery of Jerusalem and rededication of the Second Temple at the beginning of the Maccabean revolt against the Seleucid Empire in the second century B.C.E.

Hazzan: Hebrew word for cantor who leads the congregation in prayer by singing and chanting.

Haggadah: The book which Jews recite at the Passover meal which tells the story of the Israelites emerging from slavery to freedom.

High Holidays: The High Holidays are Rosh Hashanah (The Jewish New Year) and Yom Kippur (The Day of Atonement).

Maimonides: Rabbi Moses ben Maimon (also known by the acronym Rambam) lived from 1138-1204. He was born in Spain and died in Egypt. He was a Jewish philosopher and physician who became one of the most prolific and important Torah scholars of the Middle Ages.

Midrash: Biblical interpretation.

Minyan: A group of ten adults gathered for a prayer service. A minyan is needed for the recitation of certain prayers.

Mitzvah: commandment.

Open Temple: A spiritual community in Venice, CA, founded and led by Rabbi Lori Shapiro which creates an open door for everyone to go on their Jewish soul journey. https://opentemple.org

Orthodox Judaism: Orthodox Judaism is the most traditional denomination of Judaism, which believes in strict observance of Jewish law. Orthodox Judaism regards Jewish law as not changing over time.

Passover: The spring Jewish holiday which celebrates the Exodus of the Israelites from slavery in Egypt and the beginning of their journey to freedom in the Promised Land (Israel). This holiday is called *Pesach* in Hebrew.

Rashi: Rabbi Shlomo Yitzchaki, a medieval, French biblical commentator.

Rosh Hashanah: The Jewish New Year celebration.

Shabbat/Shabbos: The Sabbath: A period of rest that Jews observe from Friday at sunset to Saturday night after sunset each week – which typically involves going to services at a synagogue and festive meals with family and friends. The Sabbath is called Shabbat in Hebrew and Shabbos in Yiddish.

Shalom: Hebrew for peace.

Shalem: Hebrew for whole.

Simchat Torah: Hebrew for the joy of the Bible. *Simchat Torah* is a holiday that typically involves dancing with the *Torah* (scrolls of the Bible) with circles of dancers holding hands around the people who are holding the *Torah* scrolls.

Sukkot: Hebrew word for booths. This festival celebrates the journey of the Israelites in the desert on the way to the Promised Land. During this eight-day holiday, Jews build and then sit, eat, and even sleep sit in huts that represent the booths that the Israelites lived in during their desert trek.

Temple Beth Am: A synagogue in Los Angeles https://www.tbala.org

Temple Beth Shalom: A synagogue in Long Beach, CA https://tbslb.org

Temple Har Shalom: A synagogue in Idyllwild, CA https://templeharshalomidyllwild.org/

Torah: Hebrew for teaching. The Torah is the Hebrew Bible (the Five Books of Moses). The Torah is traditionally written on a scroll of parchment which is called a Torah scroll and kept in an ark at a synagogue.

Torah portion: In Jewish tradition, the Torah (the Five Books of Moses) is divided into 54 Torah portions, and one or two portions is assigned to each week of the year. The spiritual premise of Judaism is that the Torah portion of each week offers insights on the events in our lives and world that take place during that week.

Tu B'av: The fifteenth day of the month of Av. This greatest holiday of the Jewish year, a holiday of love, when women would dance in the vineyard and would find husbands.

Tzaraat: A disease described in the book of Leviticus that can take many forms. This ailment can turn skin white and scaly. The affliction can also manifest in clothing or even a house as a form of mold or mildew.

Yom Kippur: Hebrew for day of repentance. This holiday which takes place ten days after Rosh Hashanah involves fasting, praying, and asking forgiveness for mistakes.

Recommended Resources

Dr. Bradley Shavit Artson, *Lessons Learned from My Cancer*, Jewish Journal, September 8-14, 2023, 16-17.
https://jewishjournal.com/commentary/opinion/362488/lessons-learned-from-my-cancer/

Video: https://youtu.be/EZZXEfTx9FU?si=2Vra2qkEGYIU8OY9

Dr. Edith Eva Eger, *The Choice: Embrace the Possible*. (New York: Scribner, 2017).

Susan Jeffers, *Feel the Fear and Do it Anyway*. (New York: Fawcett Books, 1987).

Kathy Harmon-Luber, *Suffering to Thriving: Your Toolkit for Navigating Your Healing Journey* (Powell, OH: Author Academy Elite, 2022),

Sherre Hirsch, *We Plan, God Laughs: 10 Steps to Finding Your Divine Path When Life is Not Turning Out Like You Wanted* (New York: Doubleday, 2008).

Ilana Grinblat

Steve Leder, *More Beautiful Than Before: How Suffering Transforms Us* (Carlsbad, CA: Hay House Inc., 2017).

Naomi Levy, *To Begin Again: The Journey Toward Comfort, Strength, and Faith in Difficult Times* (New York: Alfred A. Knopf, 1998).

Naomi Levy, *Hope Will Find You: My Search for the Wisdom to Start Waiting and Start Living* (New York: Harmony Books, 2010).

Naomi Levy, *Talking with God: Personal Prayers for Times of Joy, Sadness, Struggle, and Celebration* (New York: Alfred A. Knopf, 2002).

Dr. Lissa Rankin, *Mind over Medicine: Scientific Proof that You Can Heal Yourself* (Carlsbad: Hay House Inc., 2014).

Jonathan Sacks, "How the Jewish People Invented Hope," https://www.myjewishlearning.com/article/how-the-jewish-people-invented-hope/

Index of Torah Portions

Bereshit (Genesis): Chapter, "Before the Biopsy," page 11.

Chapter, "Just Breathe," page 75.

Chapter, "My Birthday Present," page 170.

Chapter, The Road Less Travelled, page 180.

Chapter, "Stubborn Revisited," pages 197-198.

Noah: Chapter, "The Hardest Part," page 17.

Chapter, "Normal," pages 210-211.

Lech Lecha (Go to Yourself): Chapter, "The Hardest Part," pages 15-18.

Vayera (And appeared): Chapter, "The Megaphone, pages 57-58.

Chapter, "Hot and Cold," pages 93.

Chapter, "What do you need?" page 153.

Chapter, "Good Days and Bad Days" page 158.

Chapter, "The Prescription," page 186.

Chapter, "Epilogue," page 228.

Vayishlach (And he sent): Chapter, "How it all Began," pages 5-6.

Vayeshev (And he settled) Chapter, "The Stranger," page 138.

Shemot (Names) Chapter, "The Decision," pages 47-48.

Ilana Grinblat

Bo (Come): Chapter, "On Worry," pages 142-143.

B'shalach (When God Sent): Chapter, "Good Days and Bad Days," pages 158-160.

Yitro: (Jethro): Chapter, "Yes and No," pages 114-115.

Ki Tissa (When You Take): Chapter, "Stubborn," page 71-72. Chapter, "Broken Open," page 87-89. Chapter, "The Missing Piece," pages 103-104. Chapter, "Dry Cleaning," page 81.

Tazria-Metsorah (Delivery/The Leper): Chapter, "In the Waiting Room," pages 22-23.

Beha'alotecha (When you raise up): Chapter. "The Power of Two," page 105.

Balak: Chapter, "The Blanket," pages 60-61.

Shelach: Chapter, "Epilogue," page 229.

Korach: Chapter, "In Between," page 150-151.

V'etchanan (And I pleaded), Chapter, "Yes and No," page 114-115. Chapter, "Broken Open Again," page 194-195.

Re'eh (See) Chapter, "Hot and Cold," page 96.

Shoftim (Judges) Chapter, "The Real Heroes," page 40.

Ki Tetse (When You Go Out) Chapter, "Relinquishing," page 188.

Ki Tavo (When You Come): Chapter, "Just Rest" page 203-204.

Endnotes

[1] Babylonian Talmud, *Berakhot* 5b.

[2] Genesis 2:22.

[3] Genesis 12:1.

[4] *Ibid.*, verse 2.

[5] Genesis 12:1.

[6] Rashi on Genesis 12:2.

[7] Genesis 12:1.

[8] Leviticus 13:39.

[9] *Ibid.*, verse 3.

[10] Aharon Yakov Greenberg, ed. *Iturei Torah* (Tel Aviv, Yavneh Publishing, 1999), vol. 4, 71.

[11] Steve Leder, *More Beautiful Than Before: How Suffering Transforms Us* (Carlsbad, CA: Hay House, Inc.), 22.

[12] Rambam's Commentary on the Mishnah, Tractate Avot, Chapter 1, Mishnah 6.

[13] Milken Community School Curriculum, "Rambam." (This curriculum provides a brief summary of Maimonides' levels of

friendship. For the full original text see Rambam's Commentary on the Mishnah, Tractate Avot 1:6.)

[14] *Ibid.*

[15] *Ibid.*

[16] *Ibid.*

[17] *Ibid.*

[18] *Iturei Torah*, vol 6, 106.

[19] Vayikra Rabbah 1:3

[20] Rabbi Myra Meskin, "The Secrets of Motherhood," American Jewish University, May 5, 2022. Mother's Day | American Jewish University (aju.edu)

[21] Genesis 21:18.

[22] Numbers 24:5.

[23] *Pirkei Avot* 2:4.

[24] Babylonian Talmud, Yoma 85b. See also Shulhan Arukh, Orah Hayyim 328:2.

[25] Margot Zemach, *It Could Always Be Worse* (New York: Scholastic Book Services, 1976).

[26] Exodus 32:9.

[27] Rabbi/Dr. David Lieber, *Etz Hayim Torah and Commentary*, (New York: The Rabbinical Assembly, 2001, 532.

[28] Exodus Rabbah 42:9.

[29] *Pirkei Avot* 2:4.

[30] Genesis 2:7.

[31] Echart Tolle, *A New Earth: Awakening to Your Life's Purpose* (New York: PLUME, 2005), 244.

[32] Sherre Hirsch, *We Plan, God Laughs: 10 Steps to Finding Your Divine Path When Life is Not Turning Out Like You Wanted* (New York: Doubleday, 2008), 114-5.

[33] Exodus 34:1.

[34] Tova Marvis, *The Book of Separation: A Memoir* (New York: Houghton Mifflin Harcourt, 2017), 217.

[35] *Mahzor Lev Shalom* (New York: The Rabbinical Assembly, 2010), 312.

[36] Babylonian Talmud, *Berakhot* 8b.

[37] Rabbi Harold Kushner, *Etz Hayim Torah and Commentary,* 540.

[38] Mitch Albom, *The Next Person You Meet in Heaven* (New York: HarperCollins Publishers, 2018), 147.

[39] Deuteronomy 11:26-28.

[40] Ecclesiastes 3:1-8.

[41] Exodus 33:19-23.

[42] *Etz Hayim*, 540.

[43] Numbers 12:13.

[44] Exodus 20:8.

[45] Deuteronomy 5:11.

[46] Rabbi Ben Tzion Shafier, "The Difference between Emunah and Bitachon," Orthodox Union, July 24, 2014. https://www.ou.org/life/inspiration/difference-emunah-bitachon/

[47] Maimonides Commentary on the Mishnah, Tractate Avot, Chapter 1: 6.

[48] Dr. Edith Eva Eger, *The Choice: Embrace the Possible*. (New York: Scribner, 2017), 38.

[49] "Blending the Notes: An Analogy for Older Adults"

[50] Kathy Harmon-Luber, *Suffering to Thriving: Your Toolkit for Navigating Your Healing Journey* (Powell, OH: Author Academy Elite, 2022), 13.

[51] *Ibid.*, p. 45.

[52] Eckhart Tolle, *The Power of Now: A Guide to Spiritual Enlightenment* (Novato, CA: New World Library, 1999) 85.

[53] *Ibid.*

[54] *Ibid.*

[55] Exodus 10:26.

[56] *Etz Hayim Torah and Commentary*, 377.

[57] Dr. Lissa Rankin, *Mind over Medicine: Scientific Proof that You Can Heal Yourself* (Carlsbad: Hay House, 2014), 150.

[58] *Ibid.*, 139.

[59] Job 14:19.

[60] *Avot de Rabi Natan* 6:2.

[61] https://aish.com/like_water_on_a_rock/

[62] *Pirkei Avot* 5:6.

[63] Psalm 118:5.

[64] Dr. David Wise, Sixty Day Home Program, Part 2, 609.

[65] *Ibid.*, 610.

[66] Numbers 12:13.

[67] Exodus 13:17.

[68] Babylonian Talmud, *Eiruvin* 53b. See Kushner, *Etz Hayim*, 399.

[69] *Ibid.*

[70] Leder, xvi.

[71] David Wolpe, *Teaching Your Children about God: A Modern Jewish Approach*, (New York: Harper Perennial, 1993), 28.

[72] Harmon-Luber, 89.

[73] Babylonian Talmud, *Ketubot* 17a.

[74] Genesis 1:26.

[75] *Bereshit Rabbah* 8:5.

[76] Psalms 85:11.

[77] Babylonian Talmud, *Gittin* 55a.

[78] Babylonian Talmud, *Zevachim* 26a.

[79] Leder, xii.

[80] "The Meaning of Gird Up Your Loins in Proverbs 31:17," *Fruitfully Living Women*," https://www.fruitfullyliving.com/gird-up-your-loins/

[81] Job 2:7.

[82] Job 38:3.

[83] Dr. David Wise, Sixty Day Home Program (New Pelvic Technologies, 2021), Part 2, 46.

[84] Genesis Rabbah 9:7.

[85] Babylonian Talmud, *Yoma* 69b.

[86] Genesis 21:18.

[87] Deuteronomy 22:2.

[88] *Ibid.*, verse 3.

[89] Deuteronomy 11:18.

[90] *Etz Hayim*, 1026.

[91] Rankin, 326.

[92] Genesis 2:2-3.

[93] *Mekhilta de Rabbi Ishmael*, translated by Jacob Lauterbach (Philadelphia: Jewish Publication Society, 1933) Tractate Bachodesh, chapter 7, Vol. 2, 255-256.

[94] Genesis 2:18.

[95] https://www.sherithisrael.org/news.html?post_id=154650

[96] Deuteronomy 28:67.

[97] *Etz Hayim*, 1157.

[98] Deuteronomy 28:2.

[99] *Etz Hayim*, 1149.

[100] Babylonian Talmud, Eiruvin 13b.

[101] Genesis 8:11.

[102] Babylonian Talmud, Shabbat 21b.

[103] Genesis 1:3.

[104] https://www.myjewishlearning.com/article/how-the-jewish-people-invented-hope/

[105] *Ibid.*

[106] Psalm 118:5.

Made in United States
Orlando, FL
26 February 2025